Christmas 2013

Dearest Nicholas,

Christmas Joy and Hope
in all circumstances.
All my love.
Groups
x ox

WE SHALL
FIGHT ON THE
BEACHES

WE SHALL FIGHT ON THE BEACHES

THE SPEECHES THAT INSPIRED HISTORY

JACOB F. FIELD

Michael O'Mara Books Limited

First published in Great Britain in 2013 by
Michael O'Mara Books Limited
9 Lion Yard
Tremadoc Road
London SW4 7NQ

ISBN: 978-1-78243-055-1 in hardback print format
ISBN: 978-1-78243-206-7 in paperback print format
ISBN: 978-1-78243-091-9 in EPub format
ISBN: 978-1-78243-092-6 in Mobipocket format

1 2 3 4 5 6 7 8 9 10

www.mombooks.com

Cover design by Patrick Knowles

Designed and typeset by Envy Design Ltd

Printed and bound by CPI Group (UK) Ltd, Croydon, CR0 4YY

CONTENTS

INTRODUCTION

Times of conflict have inspired some of the most memorable speeches in history. In turn, rhetoric has launched wars, acting as a prelude to violence. Pope Urban II's address at Clermont in 1095 initiated the Crusades. His promise that 'all who die . . . shall have immediate remission of sins' was instrumental in persuading tens of thousands to become Crusaders and led to over two centuries of warfare. The power of speech has driven people to fight for glory, victory, or survival; it has shaped the outcome of wars and framed how they are viewed by posterity. President Abraham Lincoln's second inaugural address, given in the final weeks of the Civil War, emphasized that slavery must be eradicated, but also that a 'just and lasting peace' be achieved between the North and South. Words as captivating as Dragutin Gavrilović's can make soldiers braver even when the odds against them are overwhelming.

We Shall Fight on the Beaches is a collection of history's most influential wartime speeches, with an exploration of their context and consequences. The speeches in this book were delivered by some of history's greatest generals and most revered heroes, as well as some of its most reviled figures. Covering every inhabited continent, these exemplary pieces of oratory range from the Athenian general Pericles's plea to his city to remember its glorious fallen warriors during the Peloponnesian War to President Ronald Reagan's exhortation to the Communists to 'Tear Down this Wall' in Berlin in 1987, during the closing years of the Cold War. Not all the speeches in this book have accompanied glorious victories. Words in defeat can be just as memorable and important. In 1936, Emperor Haile Selassie of Ethiopia addressed the League of Nations, appealing for condemnation of Italy's conquest of his country. Despite receiving no support, his speech has become a byword for the rights of sovereign nations for security against foreign invasion and aggression.

This book is named after a line from a Winston Churchill speech given in 1940, when he had just become Prime Minister and it appeared that the

United Kingdom and the Allies were powerless to stop the Nazi tide. Churchill's defiant words are iconic because they show how words can galvanize a nation behind an inspirational leader. *We Shall Fight on the Beaches* reveals the undeniable power of the spoken word to rouse and console, to celebrate and eulogize. In victory or defeat, words in wartime have left an indelible mark on not only the history of warfare, but on the history of the world itself.

Jacob Field, 2013

431 BC
FUNERAL ORATION

PERICLES
(*c.* 4 9 5 – 4 2 9 B C)

Pericles came to power in 461 BC as leader of the democratic, populist faction and was Athens' figurehead during the city's 'golden age' of political and cultural influence. Athens itself was the major power centre in Greece, heading an alliance of city states called the Delian League. Its only rival was Sparta, a militant oligarchy that led the Peloponnesian League. Tensions between the cities led to the First Peloponnesian War (460–445 BC), which ended in stalemate, and a truce was signed.

Inevitably, given both Athens and Sparta wanted to be the dominant power, war broke out again in 431 BC. The Spartans raided the countryside around Athens, plundering and razing the farms there. Fortunately,

Pericles had been able to persuade the inhabitants of the region to seek refuge inside Athens' formidable walls. And, as Athens and her allies were more powerful at sea, Pericles avoided open battle on land, where Sparta and her allies were superior.

As the first year of the war ended, Pericles gave a funeral oration in a public ceremony to honour the war dead. Recorded by the historian Thucydides, the speech remembers the greatness of Athens.

——THE SPEECH——

Such was the end of these men; they were worthy of Athens, and the living need not desire to have a more heroic spirit, although they may pray for a less fatal issue. The value of such a spirit is not to be expressed in words. Anyone can discourse to you for ever about the advantages of a brave defense, which you know already. But instead of listening to him I would have you day by day fix your eyes upon the greatness of Athens, until you become filled with the love of her; and when you are impressed by the spectacle of her glory, reflect that this empire has been acquired by men who knew their duty and had the courage to do it, who in the hour of conflict had the fear of dishonour always present to them, and who, if ever they failed in an enterprise, would not allow their virtues to be lost to their country, but freely gave their lives to her as the fairest offering which they could present at her feast. The sacrifice which they collectively made was individually repaid to them; for they received again each one for himself a praise which grows not old, and the noblest of all tombs, I speak not of that in which their remains are laid, but of that in which their glory survives, and is proclaimed always and on every fitting occasion both in word and deed. For the whole earth is the tomb of famous men; not only are they commemorated by columns and inscriptions in their own country, but in foreign lands there dwells also an unwritten memorial of them, graven not on stone but in the hearts of men.

—— THE CONSEQUENCES ——

In 430 BC, Sparta raided Athens' countryside again. Pericles continued to avoid committing troops to battle on land, preferring to concentrate on naval war. This approach was not universally popular in Athens, with many wanting Pericles to adopt a more aggressive policy.

Then, disaster struck as a plague epidemic wiped out 30,000 of the city's inhabitants. Athens' manpower was drastically reduced. During the uproar, Pericles faced both public opposition and internal scheming from his political opponents. He was briefly stripped of his office as military leader of Athens, but managed to regain the position in 429 BC. The reverse of fortune was short-lived. That year, Pericles lost two of his sons to the plague, before falling victim himself.

Pericles' successors quickly reversed his defensive strategy, launching direct attacks on Sparta. With both sides exhausted from fighting, a peace treaty was signed between Athens and Sparta in 421 BC. Six years later, Athens re-entered the war when it launched an expedition to assist its allies in Sicily. Unfortunately it was wholly annihilated by 413 BC, leaving Athens vulnerable to Spartan attacks and raids. The decisive action of the war came in 405 BC, when the once-mighty Athenian fleet was destroyed at the Battle of Aegospotami. Athens was forced to surrender the next year. Sparta was the leading power in Greece.

First Philippic

In the mid-fourth century BC, the northern Greek kingdom of Macedon was growing to become the dominant power in the region. Macedon's king, Philip II, had won a series of victories that saw his rule expand south towards Athens. The two states had been at war since 357 BC, but Macedon was increasingly holding the upper hand.

In 351 BC, the politician Demosthenes (384–322 BC) made a speech to the Athenian popular assembly calling for their resistance in the face of the Macedonian threat. Demosthenes urged each Athenian citizen to 'act where his duty bids him, and where his services can be of use to his country'. Unless Athens was adequately prepared for war, he claimed, 'the future must be evil, unless you give heed and are ready to do your duty'.

Despite Demosthenes' passion, his exhortations proved fruitless: Philip's armies won victory after victory, culminating in their 338 BC triumph at Chaeronea, which left them the dominant force in Greece. Athens was no longer an independent city state.

326 BC
ADDRESS AT
HYDASPES RIVER

ALEXANDER THE GREAT
(356-323 BC)

By the age of thirty, Alexander the Great had carved out one of the largest empires in history, extending from Greece to India. In 336 BC, he succeeded his father as ruler of the kingdom of Macedon, the dominant power in Greece. His ambitions did not end there. Alexander aimed to conquer the great Persian Empire, which stretched from North Africa to Central Asia.

In 334 BC, his army crossed into Persian territory and, after a string of victories, he was master of Asia Minor, the Levant and Egypt. Three years later, Alexander masterminded his decisive triumph over Persia at the Battle of Gaugamela, in modern-day Iraq. Despite being outnumbered two-to-one, Alexander routed his foes. The Persian king Darius III fled and was later murdered by one of his governors.

His thirst for conquest unsated, Alexander invaded the Indian subcontinent in 326 BC. After a series of difficult battles, he faced a local king, Porus, on the banks of the Hydaspes River in modern-day Punjab. The ensuing battle was hard-fought, but the Greeks won through. Alexander wanted to press on east, cross the River Ganges, and conquer more lands, but his men refused to go any further. Stung, Alexander delivered this speech.

—— THE SPEECH ——

I observe, gentlemen, that when I would lead you on a new venture you no longer follow me with your old spirit. I have asked you to meet me that we may come to a decision together: are we, upon my advice, to go forward, or, upon yours, to turn back?

[. . .]

Come, then; add the rest of Asia to what you already possess — a small addition to the great sum of your conquests. What great or noble work could we ourselves have achieved had we thought it enough, living at ease in Macedon, merely to guard our homes,

accepting no burden beyond checking the encroach-
ment of the Thracians on our borders, or the Illyrians
and Triballians, or perhaps such Greeks as might prove
a menace to our comfort? I could not have blamed you
for being the first to lose heart if I, your commander,
had not shared in your exhausting marches and your
perilous campaigns; it would have been natural enough
if you had done all the work merely for others to reap
the reward. But it is not so. You and I, gentlemen, have
shared the labour and shared the danger, and the
rewards are for us all. The conquered territory belongs
to you; from your ranks the governors of it are chosen;
already the greater part of its treasure passes into your
hands, and when all Asia is overrun, then indeed I will
go further than the mere satisfaction of our ambitions:
the utmost hopes of riches or power which each one of
you cherishes will be far surpassed, and whoever wishes
to return home will be allowed to go, either with me or
without me. I will make those who stay the envy of
those who return.

—— THE CONSEQUENCES ——

Despite Alexander's eloquence, honed during his
studies under his childhood tutor Aristotle, he was
unable to persuade his armies to advance further east.
Instead, they turned south and marched homewards.

The Hydaspes marked the eastern limit of Alexander's conquests.

Why was Alexander, an inspirational leader who fought side-by-side with his men, unable to rouse his troops? First, they had been away from Greece for years and were desperate to see their homeland and enjoy the plunder from their numerous victories. Second, they were exhausted – in the battle against Porus they had faced war elephants and heavy rain. Third, there was tension between Alexander and some of his officers due to his adoption of Persian dress and customs, as well as his recruitment of Persians.

Alexander himself would never see his homeland again. He settled in the great city of Babylon and died after a fever in June, 323 BC, amid rumours he was poisoned. Alexander's empire ruptured into separate realms, as his senior officers battled for pre-eminence. Despite the break-up of his conquests, Alexander's greatness is undoubted. Undefeated in war, he had carved out an empire spanning three continents.

The Second Oration Against Catiline

Marcus Tullius Cicero (106–43 BC) was ancient Rome's greatest orator. In 63 BC, he became consul. During his term, Cicero delivered his most famous speeches: the Catiline Orations. Catiline was a senator who had raised an army of disgruntled veterans and Gauls. He sought to assassinate Cicero and overthrow the Republic. Cicero heard news of the threat and on 8 November, he called a meeting of the Senate at which he denounced Catiline, who was present at the assembly. Publicly shamed, Catiline fled Rome to meet his rebel army.

The next day, Cicero delivered a second oration, telling the people of Rome that Catiline had fled and that now 'no injury will now be prepared against these walls within the walls themselves by that monster and prodigy of wickedness'. In fighting the plot, Cicero promised to ensure that 'no good man shall fall, and that you may all be saved by the punishment of a few'. Conspirators in Rome were put to death and Catiline himself was killed leading his rebels against a Roman army.

218 BC
ADDRESS TO HIS
SOLDIERS

HANNIBAL

(2 4 7 – 1 8 3/1 B C)

Hannibal was ancient Rome's most formidable enemy. He was a general for the Carthaginian Empire, which centred on modern-day Tunisia and stretched across North Africa, southern Spain, Sardinia and Corsica. From the mid-third century BC, Carthage vied with Rome for dominance of the West Mediterranean. Hannibal became commander-in-chief of the Carthaginian armies in 221 BC and moved to extend Carthage's influence in Spain, bringing them into conflict with Rome.

With tensions between Carthage and Rome on the increase and war certain, Hannibal launched a daring pre-emptive strike in the heart of Roman territory. In 218 BC, he left Spain with an army of over 100,000 men and thirty-seven war elephants. He fought his way through the Pyrenees and southern Gaul, and after five months reached the Alps. No army had ever crossed the Alps in winter, but Hannibal was undaunted. Even with his elephants, he and his men traversed the Alps in just fifteen days. Rome was forced to cancel plans to invade Carthage, to repel the invaders. To make matters worse, some Gallic tribes in northern Italy had revolted against Roman rule and had allied with Hannibal. As Hannibal was preparing to meet the army sent to destroy him, he called an assembly of his soldiers and allies.

—— THE SPEECH ——

Here, soldiers, where you have first met the enemy, you must conquer or die: and the same fortune which compels you to fight, holds out to you prizes of victory.

[. . .]

On whatever side I turn my eyes, I see spirit and firmness; a veteran body of infantry, cavalry composed of the most gallant nations; you our most brave and faithful allies, and you, Carthaginians, ready to fight in the cause of your country, and at the same time with the justest resentment. We are the assailants in the war, and are carrying an invasion into Italy; we shall fight therefore with so much the greater boldness and courage, as he who makes the attack has ever more confidence and spirit, than he who stands on the defensive.

[. . .]

For your part, necessity obliges you to be brave; and, since every mean between victory and death is sunk out of reach, you must resolve to conquer, or should fortune be unfavourable, to meet death in battle rather than in flight. If this determination be firmly fixed in every one of your breasts, I affirm again, you are conquerors. The immortal gods never gave to man a more invigorating incentive to conquest.

—— THE CONSEQUENCES ——

Hannibal scattered the Roman army sent to repel him. The majority of the Gallic tribes in northern Italy then joined his cause and he won several major victories over Rome. Subsequently, Rome adopted a policy of avoiding pitched battles in favour of persistent attacks on Hannibal's armies. This 'Fabian Strategy' (named after its inventor Fabius Maximus) failed in dislodging Hannibal from Italy, so Rome decided to meet him in the field once more.

In August 216 BC, Hannibal won his most famous victory at the Battle of Cannae, destroying most of an 80,000-strong Roman army. Rome declared a national day of mourning, as many cities in southern Italy opted to join Hannibal's cause.

After Cannae, however, Rome readopted Fabian tactics and, without adequate support from home or his Italian allies, Hannibal lost impetus. In 203 BC, he was recalled to Carthage to fight off an invading Roman army. In October the following year, he met the Romans at Zama (modern-day Tunis), where Scipio Africanus's army won a stunning victory.

In the aftermath of the war, Hannibal entered into Carthaginian politics. He became so successful as a statesman that Rome demanded he be surrendered to them. Rather than be handed over, Hannibal went into exile in 195 BC, entering the service of various kings in the Near East and Asia Minor. Eventually, the Romans persuaded the King of Bithynia (in Asia Minor) to give him up. Hannibal refused to be captured and committed suicide.

48 BC
ADDRESS BEFORE THE
BATTLE OF PHARSALUS

JULIUS CAESAR
(100–44 BC)

Julius Caesar's actions were fundamental to the fall of the Roman Republic and its replacement with an imperial system. In 58 BC, after a one-year term as consul (the Republic's highest elected office), Caesar departed Rome to serve as a governor in Gaul. There, he launched an aggressive campaign to conquer Gallic tribes. He crossed into Britain in 55 BC, but was forced to abandon his campaign there in order to quell unrest in Gaul. Three years later, Caesar was victorious over a huge Gallic army at the Battle of Alesia. This gave Rome control over the whole of Gaul and won Caesar enormous wealth and prestige, as well as the respect and loyalty of his legions. However, his victories unsettled many in Rome's Senate, who, led by the influential politician Pompey, believed he had grown too powerful and ordered him to disband his army and return to Rome. Caesar refused.

On 10 January 49 BC, Caesar led his army across the Rubicon River, the northern frontier of Italy proper. It was forbidden to lead armies into Italy, as they could be used to seize power in Rome. This was exactly what Caesar intended. He knew his action would plunge Rome into civil war, and as he crossed the Rubicon, he proclaimed, 'the die is cast'. The senatorial opposition fled Rome, allowing Caesar to claim the city before marching to Spain to quell the opposition forces there. In order to fully consolidate his position, Caesar had to defeat Pompey, who had raised an army in Greece and was encamped in the city of Dyrrachium. They met on 10 July 48 BC, and Caesar only narrowly avoided defeat, retreating before he could be routed. Despite this, Caesar's legions remained loyal to him. Outnumbered two-to-one and running low on supplies, his army met Pompey's forces on 9 August at Pharsalus. Before battle, Caesar gave a rousing speech to his men.

—— THE SPEECH ——

My friends, we have already overcome our more formidable enemies, and are about to encounter not hunger and want, but men. This day will decide everything. Remember what you promised me at Dyrrachium. Remember how you swore to each other in my presence that you would never leave the field except as conquerors. These men, fellow-soldiers, are the same that we have come to meet from the Pillars of Hercules, the same men who gave us the slip from Italy. They are the same who sought to disband us without honours, without a triumph, without rewards, after the toils and struggles of ten years, after we had finished those great wars, after innumerable victories, and after we had added 400 nations in Spain, Gaul and Britain to our country's sway. I have not been able to prevail upon them by offering fair terms, nor to win them by benefits. Some, you know, I dismissed unharmed, hoping that we should obtain some justice from them. Recall all these facts to your minds today, and if you have any experience of me, recall also my care for you, my good faith, and the generosity of my gifts to you.

[. . .]

Before all else, in order that I may know that you are mindful of your promise to choose victory or death, throw down the walls of your camp as you go out to battle and fill up the ditch, so that we may have no place of refuge if we do not conquer, and so that the enemy may see that we have no camp and know that we are compelled to encamp in theirs.

—THE CONSEQUENCES—

The battle proved a defiant success for Caesar. His men claimed Pompey's camp and supplies. Pompey fled to Egypt with Caesar in pursuit. As Pompey's galley docked, Pharaoh Ptolemy XIII sent a boat to bring him ashore. Pompey believed he was being brought to a meeting but instead he was murdered and decapitated. Ptolemy hoped this act would win Caesar's favour in support of his dynastic struggle with his sister Cleopatra, but his plan backfired. When Ptolemy presented Pompey's head, Caesar was outraged, as he had hoped to pardon Pompey. Caesar instead backed Cleopatra and had Ptolemy deposed. Caesar and Cleopatra became lovers.

In 45 BC, Caesar returned to Rome after putting down the last remnants of his opposition in the Middle East, North Africa and Spain. He was then appointed dictator for life. Caesar's position appeared impregnable and his power total. However, many in the Senate believed Caesar was too powerful, and plotted to assassinate him. On 15 March 44 BC, the conspirators surprised Caesar as he took his seat in the Senate. He attempted to defend himself with a stylus, but was stabbed twenty-three times. In the aftermath of the assassination, Octavian, Caesar's grandnephew and heir, came to power with Mark Antony, Caesar's most important lieutenant. Octavian would go on to become the first Roman Emperor, ruling under the name Augustus.

1066

BE YE THE AVENGERS
OF NOBLE BLOOD

WILLIAM THE CONQUEROR
(1028–87)

William, Duke of Normandy, was directly descended from Rollo, a Viking warrior who had carved out the duchy in 911. The kings of England had close ties to Normandy. In 1002, Emma, William's great-aunt, had married King Æthelred of England and bore him two sons, Alfred and Edward. The family were forced into exile in Normandy when King Cnut of Denmark seized the English throne. When Alfred visited England in 1036, he was captured, blinded and died in captivity under the orders of Godwin, the Earl of Wessex – a powerful English nobleman.

In 1042, Edward, who became known as 'The Confessor' because of his pious and holy nature, returned to England and claimed the throne. He married Edith,

Godwin's daughter, but the couple had no children and no obvious heir. William claimed that Edward had promised him the throne, yet, when Edward died in January 1066, his brother-in-law, Harold Godwinson, succeeded him. William began making preparations to invade England and seize the throne for himself.

To complicate matters, there was yet another claimant to the throne: Harald Hardrada, the King of Norway, who invaded Yorkshire. Harold's army defeated and killed him at the Battle of Stamford Bridge on 25 September. But Harold had no time to savour his victory. On 28 September, William and his fleet landed in England. Harold had to quickly march his armies south to face his rival. The English and Norman armies drew up against each other near Hastings on 14 October. William delivered a speech to his men, exhorting them to remember the perfidy of the English, and the illustrious martial history of their Viking ancestors.

—— THE SPEECH ——

Normans! Bravest of nations! I have no doubt of your courage, and none of your victory, which never by any chance or obstacle escaped your efforts. If indeed you had, once only, failed to conquer, there might be a need now to inflame your courage by exhortation; but your native spirit does not require to be roused.

[. . .]

Let any one of the English whom, a hundred times, our predecessors, both Danes and Normans, have defeated in battle, come forth and show that the race of Rollo ever suffered a defeat from his time until now, and I will withdraw conquered. Is it not, therefore, shameful that a people accustomed to be conquered, a people ignorant of war, a people even without arrows, should proceed in order of battle against you, my brave men? Is it not a shame that King Harold, perjured as he was in your presence, should dare to show his face to you? It is amazing to me that you have been allowed to see those who, by a horrible crime, beheaded your relations and Alfred my kinsman, and that their own heads are still on their shoulders. Raise your standards, my brave men, and set neither measure nor limit to your merited rage. May the lightning of your glory be seen and the thunders of your onset heard from east to west, and be ye the avengers of noble blood.

—— THE CONSEQUENCES ——

Harold's English army held the high ground at Hastings. By maintaining a disciplined defensive line, they fought off the furious Norman attack. But the day turned as some of William's men retreated. When

English troops gave chase, it threw their formation into disorder. William seized the opportunity to launch another advance, ordering his archers to fire their arrows upwards so they would rain down on the English. After several hours of fighting, the English had become exhausted, and gaps opened up in their lines. Many of their most influential leaders and nobles were killed, including Harold's brothers. Victory was William's when Harold himself was killed. Some historians believe he was struck in the eye with an arrow, or that Norman knights rode him down and hacked him to death. With his rival dead, William marched to London and claimed the throne. He was crowned on Christmas Day.

William consolidated his power by crushing any opponents, granting his supporters lands in England, and building a series of fortifications and castles, including the Tower of London. In 1085, he ordered a comprehensive survey of all of the landholdings in England – known as the Domesday Book.

William died in 1087. His sons Robert and William succeeded him in Normandy and England, respectively. Since the Conquest, all subsequent monarchs of England have been William's descendants.

1095

SPEECH AT THE COUNCIL OF CLERMONT

POPE URBAN II
(1042–99)

The series of religious wars known as the Crusades
was one of the defining ongoing conflicts of the
medieval world. One man's words were responsible for
inspiring a wave of religious fervour that swept across
Europe, leading to centuries of warfare. That man was
Pope Urban II, born in France in 1042 as Otto de
Lagery. He was a follower of the great reformer Pope
Gregory VII, and was himself elected pope in 1088.

In 1095, the Byzantine emperor Alexios I sent an
ambassador to Urban asking for help in his war against the
Turks. Byzantium had recently lost control of Anatolia to
the opposition, and Alexios, who was nearly bankrupt,
was in desperate need of soldiers from Western Europe to
serve in his armies. The Turks had also made advances in

the Holy Land, which had disrupted Christian pilgrimage routes to the holiest of cities, Jerusalem.

Urban called a Council at Clermont in 1095. So many clergy and nobles attended that they were forced to hold meetings outside of the city in the open air. On 27 November, Urban delivered a speech exhorting the faithful to join the struggle against the Turks. The chronicler Fulcher of Chartres, who was present at Clermont, recorded his words.

—— THE SPEECH ——

Although, O sons of God, you have promised more firmly than ever to keep the peace among yourselves and to preserve the rights of the church, there remains still an important work for you to do. Freshly quickened by the divine correction, you must apply the strength of your righteousness to another matter which concerns you as well as God. For your brethren who live in the east are in urgent need of your help, and you must hasten to give them the aid which has often been promised them.

[. . .]

On this account I, or rather the Lord, beseech you as Christ's heralds to publish this everywhere and to persuade all people of whatever rank, foot-soldiers and knights, poor and rich, to carry aid promptly to those Christians and to destroy that vile race from the lands of our friends. I say this to those who are present, it meant also for those who are absent. Moreover, Christ commands it. All who die by the way, whether by land or by sea, or in battle against the pagans, shall have immediate remission of sins.

[. . .]

Behold! On this side will be the sorrowful and poor, on that, the rich; on this side, the enemies of the Lord, on that, his friends. Let those who go not put off the journey, but rent their lands and collect money for their expenses; and as soon as winter is over and spring comes, let them eagerly set out on the way with God as their guide.

— THE CONSEQUENCES —

Urban then toured France, preaching the Crusade, and sent others to spread the message across Europe. Tens of thousands rushed to take the cross, hoping their actions would lead to the remission of their sins and instant entry into Heaven. Urban set the official departure date from Europe as 15 August 1096.

This was too late for some. A preacher called Peter the Hermit had gathered together a motley and ill-equipped 'army' of 40,000 men, women and children, known as the People's Crusade. Riven by quarrels, they steadily lost men as they walked towards the Holy Land. In October, a Turkish army ambushed them, massacring most of their number and enslaving many children. A small number survived to form a group called the Tafurs. They were barefoot and filthy, living on roots and even the roasted corpses of enemies.

Meanwhile, the Princes' Crusade, which was led by powerful noblemen and included thousands of knights, had left Europe on schedule. They arrived at Constantinople by April 1097. Rather than serve Alexios directly or fight the Turks in Anatolia, they advanced towards Jerusalem. Their first major victory was the conquest of the city of Antioch in June 1098. The Crusaders arrived on the outskirts of Jerusalem on 7 June 1099. They captured the holy city on 15 July, but there was nothing holy about what followed – the Crusaders brutally sacked Jerusalem, destroying mosques, and massacring Muslims and Jews. They formed a Christian kingdom there under the French nobleman, Godfrey of Bouillon.

Urban, the man who had set the Crusades in motion, died a fortnight after Jerusalem was captured. Since the news had not yet reached Italy, he would never know of the Crusaders' success.

1187
THE RECOVERY OF
JERUSALEM

SALADIN
(1137/8–1193)

S alah ad-Din Yusuf ibn Ayyub, better known in the
West as Saladin (from the first part of his name,
which means 'Righteousness of the Faith'), was one of
the greatest military leaders of the medieval world. He
was the founder of the Ayyubid Dynasty, which under
his rule became the dominant power in the Near East.
As a young man, Saladin served the ruler of Syria, Nur
ad-Din. Politics and alliances in the twelfth-century
Near East were not a simple matter of Crusaders
against Muslims. Both fought among each other, and
were not reluctant to make alliances with those of a
different faith.

In 1169, Nur ad-Din sent Saladin to Egypt, whose
Muslim ruler had previously allied with the Christian
king of Jerusalem. Saladin made sure Egypt did not fall

under enemy control, and he won power there, becoming its sultan in 1171. When Nur ad-Din died in 1174, Saladin decided to conquer his former master's land. He fought off rivals, both Muslim and Crusader, to win control of Syria. He added territory in Yemen, Arabia and Mesopotamia to his conquests. Once he had fully established himself as the master of his realm, Saladin decided to capture the Crusader lands.

On 4 July 1187, Saladin's armies completely destroyed a massed Crusader army at the Battle of Hattin. His rousing victory robbed the Crusaders of all of their best leaders and knights, and left Jerusalem largely defenseless. Refugees had swarmed into the city as Saladin had advanced, and it was seriously overcrowded and running low on supplies. Most fighting men had been lost at Hattin so young men were armed and silver was stripped from churches to pay for weapons. Saladin was determined to conquer the city, which was a holy place for Muslims as much as it was for Jews and Christians. He marched on Jerusalem that September.

—— THE SPEECH ——

If God blesses us by enabling us to drive His enemies out of Jerusalem, how fortunate and happy we would be! For Jerusalem has been controlled by the enemy for ninety-one years, during which time God has received nothing from us here in the way of adoration. At the same time, the zeal of the Muslim rulers to deliver it languished. Time passed, and so did many [in different] generations, while the Franks succeeded in rooting themselves strongly there. Now God has reserved the merit of its recovery for one house, the house of the sons of Ayyub, in order to unite all hearts in appreciation of its members.

—— THE CONSEQUENCES ——

On hearing these words, Saladin's men were even more determined to recover Jerusalem, which had been in Christian hands since 1099. The city was well defended by stout walls, but Saladin brought them down using catapults. There was some fighting but, with the situation hopeless, Jerusalem's leaders decided to surrender. Saladin had won Jerusalem back, along with most of the other Crusader lands. The only major place to hold out was the coastal city of Tyre, in modern-day Lebanon.

Saladin's successes led to the declaration of the Third Crusade in 1189. In 1191, King Philip Augustus of France and Richard the Lionheart arrived with sizeable armies. Their first act was to retake the vital port of Acre, in modern-day Israel. The Crusaders, led by Richard, imprisoned the garrison. Saladin rushed to negotiate their surrender. Despite agreeing a ransom, Richard, eager to try to capture Jerusalem himself, ordered the slaughter of the 2,700 unarmed men. Despite his initial success, Richard was unable to decisively defeat Saladin or come close to retaking Jerusalem.

In 1192, a peace treaty was agreed. Jerusalem remained in Saladin's hands but it was to be open to Christian pilgrims. The only Crusader lands left were a narrow strip along the coast from Tyre to Jaffa, with its capital at Acre. Saladin, despite retaining Jerusalem, was unhappy with the continued Crusader presence in the region.

Before he could act to address the problem, Saladin died of a fever on 4 March 1193, in Damascus. His lands were split between members of his family. They argued and warred among themselves, steadily losing the realms built up by their predecessor. Despite the short life of his empire, Saladin is remembered by Muslims and Christians alike as a chivalrous and honourable man, and a fearless and inspirational leader.

1453
THE FINAL STAND

EMPEROR CONSTANTINE XI
(1404–53)

The Byzantine Empire was a continuation of the Roman Empire. Its capital Constantinople inherited Rome's mantle of imperial prestige and was the centre of the Orthodox Church. The expansion of the Ottoman Empire from the fourteenth century had come at the cost of former Byzantine possessions. The Ottomans swept away all opposition, conquering lands from the Middle East to the Balkans. Constantinople was virtually all that survived of Byzantium and its mighty fortifications meant it remained a Christian island in the Muslim Ottoman Empire.

In 1449, Constantine XI succeeded his brother John VIII as emperor. His rule faced the ultimate test when the Ottoman sultan, Mehmed II, decided to conquer

Constantinople. Mehmed built fortresses on either side of the Bosphorus to control sea traffic, and armed himself with powerful artillery. Constantine desperately prepared the city for the siege, stockpiling food and making repairs to the heavy walls. He appealed to Christian Europe to send him men, but only a few hundred answered the call. When the siege began in spring 1453, Mehmed led an army of 100,000; Constantine could only muster 8,000. Nevertheless, initial Ottoman attacks were driven back. As the siege continued, the fall of the city appeared inevitable. Constantine rallied his men with the following speech.

—— THE SPEECH ——

. . . The hour has come: the enemy of our faith wishes to oppress us even more closely by sea and land with all his engines and skill to attack us with the entire strength of this siege force, as a snake about to spew its venom; he is in a hurry to devour us, like a savage lion. For this reason, I am imploring you to fight like men with brave souls, as you have done from the beginning up to this day, against the enemy of our faith. I hand over to you my glorious, famous, respected, noble city, the shining Queen of cities, our homeland. You know well, my brothers, that we have four obligations in common, which force us to prefer death over survival:

first, our faith and piety; second, our homeland; third, the emperor anointed by the Lord; and fourth, our relatives and friends.

[. . .]

This wretch of a Sultan has besieged our city up to now for fifty-seven days with all his engines and strength; he has relaxed the blockade neither day nor night, but, by the grace of Christ, our Lord, who sees all things, the enemy has often been repelled, up to now, from our walls with shame and dishonour. Yet now too, my brothers, feel no cowardice, even if small parts of our fortifications have collapsed from the explosions and engine missiles, as you can see, we made all possible, necessary repairs. We are placing all hope in the irresistible glory of God. Some have faith in armament, others in cavalry, might and numbers, but we believe in the name of our Lord, our God and Saviour, and second, in our arms and strength granted to us by divine power.

[. . .]

My fellow soldiers, prepare yourselves, be firm, and remain valiant, for the pity of God. Take your example from the few elephants of the Carthaginians and how they dispersed the numerous cavalry of the Romans with their noise and appearance. If one dumb beast put another to flight, we, the masters of horses and animals, can surely even do better against our advancing enemies, since they are dumb animals, worse even than pigs. Present your shield, swords, arrows and spears to them, imagining that you are a hunting party after wild boars, so that the impious may learn that they are dealing not with dumb animals but with their lords and masters, the descendants of the Greeks and the Romans.

[. . .]

Now he [the Sultan] wants to enslave and throw the yoke upon the Mistress of Cities, our holy churches, where the Holy Trinity was worshipped, where the Holy Ghost was glorified in hymns, where angels were heard praising in chant the deity of and the incarnation of God's word, he wants to turn into shrines of his blasphemy, shrines of the mad and false Prophet, Mohammed, as well as into stables for his horses and camels.

Consider then, my brother and comrades-in-arms, how the commemoration of our death, our memory, fame and freedom can be rendered eternal.

—— THE CONSEQUENCES ——

The emperor was true to his promise of death or glory. He had rebuffed all of Mehmed's attempts to negotiate a peaceful surrender, even when the sultan offered to spare his life and grant him lands in Greece. On 29 May, the Ottomans launched a furious assault by sea and land. Their men swarmed into Constantinople as its fortifications crumbled. Constantine personally led a countercharge through a breach in the walls, but the day was lost. He was cut down in the fighting: the last Byzantine Emperor was dead. In the chaos of the battle, his body was never reliably found; he is thought to have been buried in a mass grave alongside the troops he had led into battle.

Constantine's worst fears were realized as Mehmed gave his men leave to sack the city for three days. They unleashed an orgy of violence and destruction, which saw 4,000 people killed, priceless treasures looted, and ancient buildings ransacked and burnt. Even more gallingly, the Hagia Sophia, Constantinople's Christian cathedral, was immediately converted to a mosque. The Pope sought to rally Christendom in a crusade to re-conquer Constantinople, but nothing came of it. The city remained in the hands of the Ottoman Empire, and became its capital.

1519
ADDRESS TO HIS CONQUISTADORS

HERNÁN CORTÉS

(1485–1547)

Hernán Cortés led the overthrow of the mighty Aztec Empire and established Spanish dominance over most of Mexico. Cortés was born into a minor Spanish noble family. He decided to leave his homeland for the New World, which Spain was just beginning to colonize. His first destination was the Caribbean island of Hispaniola.

Despite the occasional dispute with other Spanish colonists, Cortés was extremely successful – first in Hispaniola, then in Cuba, winning both land and fortune.

In 1518, the Governor of Cuba, Diego Veláquez, put Cortés in charge of an expedition to explore and colonize Mexico, dominated by the Aztec Empire. Cortés spent his own money fitting out and arming the expedition, which had eleven ships, 110 mariners and 553 soldiers. But at the last minute, Veláquez, who had previously argued with Cortés, changed his mind and ordered him not to leave. In February 1519, Cortés decided to defy his superior and continue with the expedition. Before they left Cuba, Cortés addressed his party.

—— THE SPEECH ——

I hold out to you a glorious prize, but it is to be won by incessant toil. Great things are achieved only by great exertions and glory was never the reward of sloth. If I have laboured hard and staked my all on this undertaking, it is for the love of that renown, which is the noblest recompense of man. But, if any among you covet riches more, be but true to me, as I will be true to you and to the occasion, and I will make you masters of such as our countrymen have never dreamed of! You are few in number, but strong in resolution; and, if this does not falter, doubt not but that the Almighty, who has never deserted the Spaniard in his contest with the infidel, will shield you, though encompassed by a cloud of enemies; for your cause is a just cause, and you are to fight under the banner of the Cross. Go forward then, with alacrity and confidence, and carry to a glorious issue the work so auspiciously begun.

Cortés and his band landed in Mexico. He ordered the sinking of his fleet to ensure against a mutiny – there would be no way home. Cortés then marched to the interior, to form a military alliance with the native Tlaxcalans, who were involved in an ongoing conflict with the Aztecs. Cortés and his allies advanced on the Aztec capital Tenochtitlan. The city was located on an island on the site of modern-day Mexico City. The Aztec Emperor Moctezuma II greeted Cortés warmly but not everyone welcomed the Spanish. As tensions rose, Cortés decided to take Moctezuma captive so he could rule the city himself. Before he could fully consolidate his position, Cortés faced another threat. His former master Veláquez, angry at Cortés's disobedience, had sent an expedition to Mexico to oppose him. Cortés rushed away to face it, leaving his deputy Pedro de Alvarado in charge.

On 10 May 1520, the Aztecs held a religious festival. Hundreds gathered at the main temple. In an unprovoked attack, Alvarado massacred them all. Tenochtitlan fell into anarchy. Cortés, who had defeated Veláquez's expedition, rushed back to Tenochtitlan but he could not restore order. The people of the city overthrew Moctezuma and revolted against the Spanish.

Cortés and his men were forced to flee the city on 1

July, with hundreds of lives lost. The Spanish called it the Noche Triste (Night of Sorrows). Undeterred, Cortés gathered his forces and led them back to Tenochtitlan to cut off the island and its supplies of food and water. Smallpox, which the Spanish had brought to Mexico, raged across the city. After eight months, on 13 August 1521, Tenochtitlan fell. The Spanish and their allies sacked the city, killing thousands, tearing down Aztec buildings and temples, and building new structures on their ruins.

With the Aztec Empire destroyed, Cortés was appointed the governor of the territory. He did not enjoy his success for long: Cortés continued to quarrel with other Spanish colonial officials and lost his position as governor in 1526. He went on to launch several other expeditions in the region, but never recovered his former success. He died in Mexico in 1547.

1588
SPEECH TO THE TROOPS
AT TILBURY

ELIZABETH I
(1533–1603)

Elizabeth I was born into a continent riven by warfare and religious dispute. Conflict between Catholics and Protestants threw Europe into confessional warfare. When Elizabeth's sister Mary died in 1558, Elizabeth succeeded her as queen. Philip, Mary's widower, wanted to marry Elizabeth. She rebutted his advances, as well as those of all other suitors, and her identity as the 'Virgin Queen' was vital to inspiring loyalty and devotion in her subjects.

Elizabeth's policies drew England into conflict with Philip. English privateers, led by Sir Francis Drake, attacked Spanish shipping and ports, disrupting the flow of precious metals from the New World that were so vital to Spain. In 1585, Elizabeth formally allied with Dutch Protestant rebels in revolt against Philip. Angered, Philip decided to overthrow Elizabeth and restore Catholicism in England.

In 1588, he sent a huge 'Armada' of ships towards the coast of Flanders, where it was to rendezvous with Spanish troops, commanded by the Duke of Parma, Spain's most successful general, and invade England. But Philip's plan went awry. The Armada was forced to harbour in Calais on 27 July, where it was attacked by English fireships. With the Armada thrown into chaos, England still faced the threat of Parma's invasion army. An army of 4,000 was mustered at Tilbury, in Essex, to protect the route into London. On 9 August, Elizabeth, mounted on a horse and wearing silver armour, addressed her troops.

—— THE SPEECH ——

My loving people. We have been persuaded by some that are careful of our safety, to take heed how we commit our selves to armed multitudes, for fear of treachery; but I assure you I do not desire to live to distrust my faithful and loving people. Let tyrants fear. I have always so behaved myself that, under God, I have placed my chiefest strength and safeguard in the loyal hearts and goodwill of my subjects; and therefore I am come amongst you, as you see, at this time, not for my recreation and disport, but being resolved, in the midst and heat of the battle, to live and die amongst you all; to lay down for my God, and for my kingdom, and my people, my honour and my blood, even in the dust. I know I have the body but of a weak and feeble woman; but I have the heart and stomach of a king, and of a king of England too, and think foul scorn that Parma or Spain, or any prince of Europe, should dare to invade the borders of my realm; to which rather than any dishonour shall grow by me, I myself will take up arms, I myself will be your general, judge and rewarder of every one of your virtues in the field. I know already, for your forwardness you have deserved rewards and crowns; and we do assure you in the word of a prince, they shall be duly paid you. In the mean time, my lieutenant general shall be in my stead, than whom never prince commanded a more noble or worthy subject; not doubting but by your obedience to my general, by your concord in the camp, and your valour in the field, we shall shortly have a famous victory over those enemies of my God, of my kingdom, and of my people.

—— THE CONSEQUENCES ——

The men at Tilbury were never called into action; Parma's army, by now ridden with disease, was unable to cross the Channel, and the Armada, chased by English ships, sailed around Scotland and Ireland, then made for home amid cold and stormy weather. Barely half of the 130 ships that had left Spain returned.

England's delivery from invasion was seen as divinely inspired. Elizabeth had special medals minted, which said, GOD BLEW, AND THEY WERE SCATTERED. 'Good Queen Bess' had emerged from the potential crisis unscathed and the defeat of the Armada was the zenith of her reign. Spain sent two more Armadas, in 1596 and 1597, but storms scattered them both. England remained safe from invasion.

On Elizabeth's death in 1603, she was succeeded by James VI of Scotland. He made peace with Spain and Protestant England was preserved.

1653
Dismissal of the Rump Parliament

Oliver Cromwell
(1599–1658)

Oliver Cromwell came to prominence as a successful cavalry commander in the English Civil War, fighting with Parliament against King Charles I. He was a natural leader, inspirational and decisive, and he became one of the most powerful Parliamentarians as they moved to victory over the Crown. Tensions rose between Parliamentarians who wanted to allow Charles to return as king with limited powers and others, dominated by the army, who wanted to rid England of its monarchy altogether.

In 1648, a group of soldiers marched to Parliament and removed the members who wanted to negotiate with Charles. The remaining members formed the Rump Parliament. With Cromwell's support, the

Rump succeeded in charging and executing Charles for treason. With the nation now a republic, Cromwell was one of the most powerful men in the country. Parliament faced continued opposition in Ireland and Scotland, and Cromwell led the armies that pacified them. When he returned to London, he found the Rump had done little to reform the nation. Tired of their endless vacillations, on 20 April 1653, he stormed into the House of Commons accompanied by several musketeers to deliver this speech.

—— THE SPEECH ——

It is high time for me to put an end to your sitting in this place, which you have dishonoured by your contempt of all virtue, and defiled by your practice of every vice. Ye are a factious crew, and enemies to all good government. Ye are a pack of mercenary wretches, and would like Esau sell your country for a mess of pottage, and like Judas betray your God for a few pieces of money. Is there a single virtue now remaining amongst you? Is there one vice you do not possess? Ye have no more religion than my horse. Gold is your God. Which of you have not bartered your conscience for bribes? Is there a man amongst you that has the least care for the good of the Commonwealth? Ye sordid prostitutes have you not defiled this sacred place, and turned the Lord's temple into a den of thieves, by your immoral principles and wicked practices? Ye are grown intolerably odious to the whole nation. You were deputed here by the people to get grievances redressed, are yourselves become the greatest grievance. Your country therefore calls upon me to cleanse this Augean stable, by putting a final period to your iniquitous proceedings in this House; and which by God's help, and the strength he has given me, I am now come to do. I command ye therefore, upon the peril of your lives, to depart immediately out of this place. Go, get you out! Make haste! Ye venal slaves be gone! So! Take away that shining bauble there, and lock up the doors. In the name of God, go!

—— THE CONSEQUENCES ——

As he ended his harangue, Cromwell snatched away the Parliamentary mace (the 'shining bauble'), the symbol of the chamber's power. Cromwell then established the 'Parliament of Saints' – a new assembly composed of men who shared his political and religious convictions – but it proved just as ineffective as its predecessor in solving the knotty problems of creating a new form of government. It dissolved itself in December 1653. A new constitution was put in place, with Cromwell as self-appointed 'Lord Protector'. But despite being the ultimate power in the land, Cromwell was unable to forge a new form of government wholly acceptable to both Parliament and the Army.

When he died in 1658, Cromwell's son Richard succeeded him as Lord Protector, but he lacked his father's authority and resigned in 1659. With no clear leadership, Charles' son Charles II was invited to return from continental exile. In 1660, he was restored as king, albeit with greatly constrained powers. Cromwell's body was dug up and posthumously executed. The corpse was hung in chains, the body flung into a pit, and the head displayed publicly in Westminster.

Speech before execution

By 1648, Charles I (1600–49) and his army of Cavaliers had been defeated by the Parliamentarian Roundheads. Charles was formally tried for being 'a tyrant, a traitor, a murderer, and a public enemy to the Commonwealth of England'. He was found guilty and sentenced to death by beheading on 27 January. The execution was to take place on 30 January 1649 in Whitehall. That afternoon, Charles walked to the scaffold, where the executioner and his assistant awaited him. Charles had donned warm clothes so he would not shiver, lest it be mistaken for fear.

Before his death, he addressed the massed crowds. He protested his innocence, claiming 'all the world knows that I never did begin a war with the two Houses of Parliament [and] . . . that I never did intent for to encroach upon their privileges.' Charles claimed to be a 'martyr of the people'. Before he put his head on the block, Charles said, 'I go from a corruptible, to an incorruptible Crown; where no disturbance can be, no disturbance in the world.' Charles tucked his hair into a cap so it would not impede the axe, and laid his neck on the block.

1716
SPEECH TO THE COUNCIL OF PERTH

JAMES FRANCIS EDWARD STUART
(1688–1766)

James Francis Edward Stuart was the Catholic heir to the British throne at a time when negative attitudes towards Catholicism were rife. A group of influential nobles offered the throne to his Protestant sister Mary, who was married to the Dutch ruler, William of Orange. In the 'Glorious Revolution', William and Mary Stuart claimed the British throne, while James and the rest of his family were exiled in France.

In 1714, Anne, the last of the Stuart dynasty, died. Her successor was George of Hanover, a German prince who was her nearest Protestant relative; but many saw James as the legitimate king.

In 1715, the Earl of Mar, a Scottish aristocrat, raised James's standard, igniting a Jacobite uprising. Mar was at first successful in taking control of central and northern Scotland, but, opposed by an army led by the Duke of Argyll, was unable to capture Edinburgh. Mar retreated north to Perth.

James landed in Scotland on 22 December to reclaim his birthright in the land he had left as an infant. Styling himself James III of England and Ireland and James VIII of Scotland, he aimed to restore the full power of the Crown in Britain. On 16 January 1716, James addressed his supporters at Perth.

—— THE SPEECH ——

I am now on your repeated invitations come among you. No other arguments need be used of the great confidence I place in your loyalty and fidelity to me, which I entirely rely on. I believe you are already convinced of my good intentions to restore the ancient laws and liberties of this kingdom; if not, I am still ready to confirm to you the assurance of doing all that can give you satisfaction therein. The great discouragements which presented, were not sufficient to deter me from coming to put myself at the head of my faithful subjects who were in arms for me; and whatever shall ensue, I shall leave no room for any complaint that I have not done the utmost they could expect from me. Let those who forget their allegiance and are negligent of their own good be answerable for the worst that may happen. For me, it will be no new thing if I am unfortunate; my whole life, even from my cradle, has shown a constant series of misfortunes; and I am prepared (if it so please God) to suffer the threats of my enemies and yours. The preparations which are making against us, will, I hope, quicken your resolutions and convince others from whom I have had assurances that it is now no time to dispute what they have to do. If otherwise, they shall by their remissness be unmindful of their own safety, I shall take it as my greatest comfort that I have acquitted myself in whatever could be expected from me. I recommend to you what is necessary to be done in the present conjecture, and, next to God, rely on your counsel and resolution.

—— THE CONSEQUENCES ——

James was not a particularly charismatic man and he found it difficult to galvanize his supporters. To make matters worse, he quickly fell ill because of the cold weather. James's welcome in Scotland turned similarly frosty. By the end of the month, with Argyll's army fast approaching, Mar led his men north of Perth. With the rising petering out and Mar's forces dwindling, James sailed back to France on 5 February. His journey to Scotland had been a failure.

There was no respite in France. He was no longer welcome at court there, as his former patron Louis XIV had died, and the new regime did not want to support James's claim. At the invitation of Pope Clement XI, James moved to Rome. He married Maria Sobieska, the granddaughter of the Polish king, and they had two sons, Charles and Henry. James, who became known as the 'Old Pretender', died in Rome in 1766.

Sermon at York Castle

James Stuart's son 'Bonnie Prince Charlie' (1720–88) landed in Scotland in 1745. Many Highland clans still supported the Jacobite cause and Charles aimed to enlist them in an attempt to overthrow the Hanoverian king, George II, and place his father on the throne. On 21 September, Charles's army entered Edinburgh. His next target was England.

In this febrile atmosphere, Thomas Herring, the Archbishop of York (1693–1757), delivered a sermon at York Castle. He stated that 'these commotions in the North are but part of a Great Plan concerted for our ruin'. Herring told his audience that they currently had 'the mild administration of a just and Protestant king'. If the revolt were successful, England would fall under Catholic, foreign, dominance, and 'we must submit to a man to govern us . . . who brings his Religion from Rome, and rules and maxims of his government from Paris and Madrid.'

Charles's army failed to advance further south than Derbyshire and, on 16 April 1746, was crushed at the Battle of Culloden. Herring, the man who had spoke out against the Jacobite threat, rose to become the Archbishop of Canterbury, an office that he held until his death in 1757.

1775
GIVE ME LIBERTY, OR
GIVE ME DEATH

PATRICK HENRY
(1736–99)

In 1765, the thirteen British colonies in North America were united in their opposition to the Stamp Act. This was a direct tax on the colonies, which levied a compulsory charge on paperwork of all kinds, from wills to playing cards. As colonists could not vote in British Parliamentary elections, they deemed it unconstitutional that they should be forced to pay a British tax. Taxation without representation, they argued, was both illegal and tyrannical. In response, a boycott of taxed British tea began in the colonies.

Patrick Henry, the son of a Scottish immigrant, had won renown in Virginia through his work as a lawyer. In 1765, he was elected to the colony of Virginia's

House of Burgesses, its main legislative body. He spearheaded the agitation against the Stamp Act and the British king. So fiery was his rhetoric that some in the chamber cried treason. Over the clamour, Henry replied, 'If this be treason, make the most of it!'

In 1773, tensions in the colonies increased when shiploads of British tea were destroyed at the Boston Tea Party. In response, Britain put Massachusetts under military rule. In 1774, each colony sent representatives, one of which was Henry, to a Continental Congress to coordinate their efforts. Henry continued to speak out against King George III and urged the colony to begin preparations for war. On 23 March 1775, Henry made his most famous speech at Saint John's Church in Richmond, Virginia.

—— THE SPEECH ——

This is no time for ceremony. The question before the house is one of awful moment to this country. For my own part, I consider it as nothing less than a question of freedom or slavery.

[. . .]

We have done everything that could be done to avert the storm which is now coming on. We have petitioned; we have remonstrated; we have supplicated; we have prostrated ourselves before the throne, and have implored its interposition to arrest the tyrannical hands of the ministry and Parliament. Our petitions have been slighted; our remonstrances have produced additional violence and insult; our supplications have been disregarded; and we have been spurned, with contempt, from the foot of the throne!

[. . .]

There is no retreat but in submission and slavery! Our chains are forged! Their clanking may be heard on the plains of Boston! The war is inevitable – and let it come! I repeat it, sir, let it come. It is in vain, sir, to extenuate the matter. Gentlemen may cry, Peace, Peace – but there is no peace. The war is actually begun! The next gale that sweeps from the north will bring to our ears the clash of resounding arms! Our brethren are already in the field! Why stand we here idle? What is it that gentlemen wish? What would they have? Is life so dear, or peace so sweet, as to be purchased at the price of chains and slavery? Forbid it, Almighty God! I know not what course others may take; but as for me, give me liberty or give me death!

—— THE CONSEQUENCES——

Henry's rousing words had the desired effect. The crowds, which reportedly included both George Washington and Thomas Jefferson, shouted, 'To Arms! To Arms!' The House of Burgesses resolved to mobilize its troops to join any war against the British.

In April 1775, the first shots of the war were fired at the Battles of Lexington and Concord. There was now open warfare between Britain and the American colonies and, on 4 July 1776, the Continental Congress declared the independence of the colonies from Britain. For most of the war, Henry was the Governor of Virginia. After the fighting ended and American independence was assured, Henry was again elected governor, serving from 1784 to 1786.

In 1799, Henry died of stomach cancer at his Virginia estate. His cry of 'Liberty or Death' would become a motto for revolutionaries the world over.

1783
THE NEWBURGH
ADDRESS

GEORGE WASHINGTON
(1732–99)

George Washington, the first, and arguably greatest, president of the United States, was commander-in-chief of the Continental Army during the Revolutionary War. At the helm, he took charge of the siege of Boston and forced the British to withdraw in March, 1776. In August, the British launched a major attack to capture New York City. Washington engaged them at the Battle of Long Island, but he was defeated and Britain captured the city. Washington rescued the situation by leading a daring nocturnal retreat across the East River, meaning losses of men and equipment were minimized.

In 1778, France entered the war on the American side, tilting the balance of the conflict and, in 1781,

Washington won an epochal victory at Yorktown, forcing a large British army to surrender. This ended major fighting in North America. The French withdrew and the British began to make overtures for peace but the American position was not wholly secure. The British navy remained in the vicinity and they still had troops stationed in New York City, Charleston, and Savannah.

After years of war, American funds were running low. The soldiers and officers of the Continental Army encamped at Newburgh (sixty miles north of New York City), unpaid for months and fearful that promises to pay pensions would not be met, began to agitate. The threat of mutiny was real and there were rumours the army might march on Congress to force the payment of their back wages. If the army rebelled, the Americans would be vulnerable to British attack. On 15 March 1783, Washington addressed a meeting of officers at Newburgh.

—— THE SPEECH ——

. . . If my conduct heretofore has not evinced to you that I have been a faithful friend to the army, my declaration of it at this time would be equally unavailing and improper. But as I was among the first who embarked in the cause of our common country.

As I have never left your side one moment, but when called from you on public duty. As I have been the constant companion and witness of your distresses, and not among the last to feel and acknowledge your merits. As I have ever considered my own military reputation as inseparably connected with that of the army. As my heart has ever expanded with joy, when I have heard its praises, and my indignation has arisen, when the mouth of detraction has been opened against it, it can scarcely be supposed, at this late stage of the war, that I am indifferent to its interests.

[. . .]

While I give you these assurances, and pledge myself in the most unequivocal manner to exert whatever ability I am possessed of in your favor, let me entreat you, gentlemen, on your part, not to take any measures which, viewed in the calm light of reason, will lessen the dignity and sully the glory you have hitherto maintained; let me request you to rely on the plighted faith of your country, and place a full confidence in the purity of the intentions of Congress.

[. . .]

By thus determining and thus acting, you will pursue the plain and direct road to the attainment of your wishes. You will defeat the insidious designs of our enemies, who are compelled to resort from open force to secret artifice. You will give one more distinguished proof of unexampled patriotism and patient virtue, rising superior to the pressure of the most complicated sufferings. And you will, by the dignity of your conduct, afford occasion for posterity to say, when speaking of the glorious example you have exhibited to mankind, 'Had this day been wanting, the world had never seen the last stage of perfection to which human nature is capable of attaining.'

—— THE CONSEQUENCES ——

Washington's words moved many of those present to tears. He had reminded them of the higher purposes and ideals of the revolution, and the sacrifices that he had made for it. The pay dispute was quickly settled and, a few weeks later, hostilities with Britain ended as they withdrew their armies from America. By the end of the year, Washington had disbanded the Continental Army and stood down as its commander-in-chief. His voluntary resignation of power was essential in enshrining the principle of civilian supremacy over the military in the protean United States.

Washington, with independence won, prepared for retirement at Mount Vernon. This was not to be. The needs of the nation robbed him of a quiet life. From 1787, he served as the president of the Constitutional Convention, which was called to decide what form of government the new nation would adopt. In 1789, he was unanimously elected as the first president of the United States of America. On Washington's death in 1799, Henry Lee, one of his wartime comrades, eulogized him as 'first in war, first in peace, and first in the hearts of his countrymen'.

1794

REPORT ON THE PRINCIPLES OF POLITICAL MORALITY

MAXIMILIEN DE ROBESPIERRE

(1758–94)

Following revolt and financial crisis in France, and the execution of King Louis XVI, the National Convention, France's governing power, set up a Committee of Public Safety. This was dominated by the radical Jacobins and their leader, Maximilien Robespierre. The Committee organized a new army, which saved France from the threat of invasion. But Robespierre still believed that harsher measures were necessary to preserve the Republic against its internal enemies. This led to the implementation of the Great Terror, which began in September 1793. A 'Law of Suspects' defined a broad range of offenses as 'counter-revolutionary', and 250,000 people were imprisoned. Many others were executed on the guillotine, often with seemingly little justification. Christianity was effectively outlawed, and priests were subject to death if discovered. On 5 February 1794, Robespierre addressed the Convention to justify the violent policies he had adopted.

—— THE SPEECH ——

In order to lay the foundations of democracy among us and to consolidate it, in order to arrive at the peaceful reign of constitutional laws, we must finish the war of liberty against tyranny and safely cross through the storms of the revolution: that is the goal of the revolutionary system which you have put in order. You should therefore still base your conduct upon the stormy circumstances in which the Republic finds itself; and the plan of your administration should be the result of the spirit of revolutionary government, combined with the general principles of democracy.

[. . .]

The French are the first people of the world who have established real democracy, by calling all men to equality and full rights of citizenship; and there, in my judgement, is the true reason why all the tyrants in league against the Republic will be vanquished.

[. . .]

We must smother the internal and external enemies of the Republic or perish, in this situation, the first maxim of your policy ought to be to lead the people by reason and the people's enemies by terror. If the mainspring of popular government in peacetime is virtue, amid revolution it is at the same time [both] virtue and terror: virtue, without which terror is fatal; terror, without which virtue is impotent. Terror is nothing but prompt, severe, inflexible justice; it is therefore an emanation of virtue.

—— THE CONSEQUENCES ——

Robespierre's words showed his total commitment to the Revolution, whatever the cost. He went further in June 1794, when he passed a law that abolished normal rules of evidence, and allowed 'moral proof' of guilt of suspects. The right of the accused to defend themselves was dissolved.

In six weeks, over 1,000 people were sent to the guillotine in Paris. The violence quickly spread across the rest of France. In total, around 40,000 people died during the Terror. The waves of violence and bloodshed turned many against Robespierre. The Convention ordered his arrest and declared him an outlaw. A band was sent to capture him in Paris. Robespierre tried to evade them by jumping out of a window, but he only succeeded in breaking both of his legs and was captured. He then attempted to commit suicide by shooting himself, but was unsuccessful.

On 28 July 1794, Robespierre and his supporters were sent to the guillotine and beheaded. The Committee of Public Safety was stripped of its powers and the Jacobins were banned; many of them were executed.

1805
SPEECH BEFORE AND AFTER THE BATTLE OF AUSTERLITZ

NAPOLEON BONAPARTE
(1769–1821)

Napoleon Bonaparte was born on the Mediterranean island of Corsica, which was ruled by France. He graduated from a military academy in 1785 and quickly rose through the ranks of the French army, becoming a general while still in his early twenties. The Revolution, which Napoleon supported, had flung France into war with neighbours hostile to her new republican regime. Napoleon won numerous victories for the nascent Republic and became increasingly more powerful. In 1799, he returned to France from campaigning in the Middle East and seized power in a coup. By 1804, he was named Emperor of the French.

The next year, Napoleon abandoned plans to invade

Britain in favour of marching east to face the allied forces of Austria and Russia. His troops, after a series of swift manoeuvres, surrounded the bulk of the Austrian army at the Bavarian town of Ulm, forcing their surrender in October. On 16 November, the French won a closely fought engagement over the allies at Hollabrunn in Austria. This was a prelude to the decisive engagement at Austerlitz (in modern-day Czech Republic) on 2 December – the first anniversary of Napoleon's coronation as emperor. Alexander I and Francis II, emperors of Russia and Austria, respectively, commanded their armies in person. Though outnumbered, Napoleon confidently addressed the men of the Grand Armée.

—— THE SPEECH ——

Soldiers: the Russian army has presented itself before you to revenge the disasters of the Austrians at Ulm. They are the same men that you conquered at Hollabrunn, and on whose flying trails you have followed. The positions which they occupy are formidable. While they are marching to turn my right, they must present their flank to your blows.

Soldiers: I will myself direct all your battalions. I will keep myself at a distance from the fire, if, with your accustomed valor, you carry disorder and confusion into the enemies' ranks. But should victory appear for a moment uncertain, you will see your Emperor expose himself to the first strokes. Victory must not be doubtful on this occasion.

[After the battle]
Soldiers: I am satisfied with you. In the Battle of Austerlitz, you have justified all that I expected from your intrepidity. You have decorated your eagles with immortal glory. An army of one hundred thousand men, commanded by the Emperors of Russia and Austria, has been, in less than four hours, either cut in pieces or dispersed. Thus, in two months the third coalition has been vanquished and dissolved. Peace can not now be far distant. But I will make only such a peace as gives us guarantee for our future, and secures rewards to our allies. When everything necessary to secure the happiness and prosperity of our country is obtained, I will lead you back to France. My people will behold you again with joy. It will be enough for one of you to say, 'I was at the battle of Austerlitz;' for all your fellow citizens to exclaim, 'There is a brave man.'

— THE CONSEQUENCES —

Napoleon's victory was total. After weakening the allied centre, the French had charged and captured the high ground; their enemies lost 27,000 men, while the French lost only 9,000. Napoleon considered Austerlitz his finest victory as a general.

When the Russians had returned home and the Austrians made peace, Napoleon commissioned the Arc de Triomphe in Paris to celebrate his victory, and gave everyone who had fought in the battle a cash bonus. Napoleon and his allies now dominated Europe.

Napoleon then set his sights on Spain, but his invasion of the Iberian Peninsula in 1807 saw the Spanish and Portuguese, aided by the Duke of Wellington's British armies, sap Napoleon's strength. His invasion of Russia in 1812 dealt a greater blow. As winter set in and he was still unable to defeat his enemies, Napoleon was forced to retreat in the bitter cold with only 120,000 remaining of his 625,000 men. He abdicated, and was exiled on the Mediterranean island of Elba.

The exile was a short one. Napoleon escaped in February 1815, and assumed leadership in France once more. But, on 18 June 1815, Napoleon suffered his ultimate defeat at the Battle of Waterloo at the hands of a massed British-Prussian army led by his nemesis, Wellington. There was to be no way back for Napoleon. He was imprisoned and exiled to the remote Atlantic island of Saint Helena, over 1,000 miles from the coast of West Africa. He never saw France again.

1819
ADDRESS AT THE CONGRESS OF ANGOSTURA

SIMÓN BOLÍVAR

(1783–1830)

From the mid-eighteenth century, Spanish lands in South America agitated for social and political reform. In the early nineteenth century, they began to fragment into numerous local 'juntas', and declared their independence from Spain. While the Spanish crown fought to keep their empire together, Simón Bolívar, a Venezuelan military leader, was determined to fight for freedom. In 1813, he secured Venezuelan independence, and the same year issued the 'Decree of War to the Death', which allowed murder and violence against civilians born in Spain who did not support South American independence. The Spanish fought back, and began to make progress in re-establishing their empire. Bolívar, as the figurehead of the fight for independence in Venezuela and Colombia, called a congress at the Venezuelan town of Angostura. In an address on 15 February 1819, he set out his ambitious aims once independence was secured.

—— THE SPEECH ——

We are not Europeans; we are not Indians; we are but a mixed species of aborigines and Spaniards. Americans by birth and Europeans by law, we find ourselves engaged in a dual conflict: we are disputing with the natives for titles of ownership, and at the same time we are struggling to maintain ourselves in the country that gave us birth against the opposition of the invaders. Thus, our position is most extraordinary and complicated. But there is more. As our role has always been strictly passive and political existence nil, we find that our quest for liberty is now even more difficult of accomplishment; for we, having been placed in a state lower than slavery, had been robbed not only of our freedom but also of the right to exercise an active domestic tyranny. We have been ruled more by deceit than by force, and we have been degraded more by vice than by superstition. Slavery is the daughter of darkness: an ignorant people is a blind instrument of its own destruction.

[. . .]

Therefore, let the entire system of government be strengthened, and let the balance of power be drawn up in such a manner that it will be permanent and incapable of decay because of its own tenuity. Precisely because no form of government is so weak as the democratic, its framework must be firmer, and its institutions must be studied to determine their degree of stability. Unless this is done, we will have to reckon with an ungovernable, tumultuous and anarchic society, not with a social order where happiness, peace and justice prevail.

—— THE CONSEQUENCES ——

Bolívar wanted to create a centralized federal state with a powerful president. Six months after his address, he won an important battle over the Spanish at Boyacá, in Colombia. In its aftermath, he established the independent federal republic of Gran Colombia and became its first president. This state covered modern-day Colombia, Panama, Venezuela, Ecuador, northern Peru and northwestern Brazil. This was not the end of his ambitions: he was determined to liberate all of Spanish South America. He helped Peru to secure its independence from Spain in 1824 and, in 1825, independent Upper Peru was renamed Bolivia in Bolívar's honour.

Despite these successes, Bolívar struggled to maintain control of Gran Colombia. Uprisings and dissent spread across the new republic, and the ambitious federal model that he had proposed at Angostura became difficult to implement. In 1828, trying to restore order, Bolívar declared himself the dictator of Gran Colombia, but, in fact, this led to further dissent and an attempt was made on his life.

Bolívar resigned from office in April 1830, exhaustedly proclaiming, 'All who served the Revolution have ploughed the sea.'

1860
ADDRESS TO HIS SOLDIERS

GIUSEPPE GARIBALDI
(1807–82)

In his twenties, Giuseppe Garibaldi had joined La Giovine Italia ('the Young Italy') movement, which wanted to unify all of Italy into a democratic republic – if necessary, by revolt. In 1834, Garibaldi participated in a failed campaign in Piedmont, in northwest Italy. He fled to France, and was sentenced to death by the Piedmontese authorities. He then emigrated to South America, where he fought in the Uruguayan Civil War.

From 1848, with a wave of revolutions sweeping across Europe, Garibaldi returned to Italy to rejoin the struggle for unification and independence. He conducted brave military campaigns to overcome the rule of the Austrian Empire, which controlled large swathes of northeastern Italy, and became the hero of the *Risorgimento* ('Resurgence'). Abandoning his republican ideals, Garibaldi swung his support behind Victor Emmanuel, the King of Sardinia. Garibaldi believed Italy could be unified, albeit into a monarchy, under Emmanuel's leadership. He raised a volunteer force and won several victories against the Austrians. In 1860, he and his 1,000 'red shirts' took Sicily. His army then advanced to Naples, turning the city over to Victor Emmanuel. Garibaldi refused any rewards for his efforts. Before returning home to his farm on Caprera, Sardinia, he addressed his men.

—— THE SPEECH ——

Yes, young men, Italy owes to you an undertaking which has merited the applause of the universe. You have conquered and you will conquer still, because you are prepared for the tactics that decide the fate of battles. You are not unworthy the men who entered the ranks of a Macedonian phalanx, and who contended not in vain with the proud conquerors of Asia. To this wonderful page in our country's history, another more glorious still will be added, and the slave shall show at last to his free brothers a sharpened sword forged from the links of his fetters.

To arms, then, all of you! All of you! And the oppressors and the mighty shall disappear like dust. You, too, women, cast away all the cowards from your embraces; they will give you only cowards for children, and you who are the daughters of the land of beauty must bear children who are noble and brave. Let timid doctrinaires depart from among us to carry their servility and their miserable fears elsewhere. This people is its own master. It wishes to be the brother of other peoples, but to look on the insolent with a proud glance, not to grovel before them imploring its own freedom. It will no longer follow in the trail of men whose hearts are foul. No! No! No!

[...]

Today, I am obliged to retire, but for a few days only. The hour of battle will find me with you again, by the side of the champions of Italian liberty. Let those only return to their homes who are called by the imperative duties which they owe to their families, and those who by their glorious wounds have deserved the credit of their country. These, indeed, will serve Italy in their homes by their counsel, by the very aspect of the scars which adorn their youthful brows. Apart from these, let all others remain to guard our glorious banners. We shall meet again before long to march together to the redemption of our brothers who are still slaves of the stranger. We shall meet again before long to march to new triumphs.

WE SHALL FIGHT ON THE BEACHES
—THE CONSEQUENCES—

Victor Emmanuel went on to win control of the Kingdom of Naples and, in 1861, he was proclaimed King of Italy. The Papal States, centred on Rome, remained independent, but under the domination of France, who stationed a garrison there. Garibaldi was determined to win Rome for Italy. In 1862, he marched on the city under the banner 'Roma o Morte' ('Rome or Death'). Victor Emmanuel was reluctant to attack Rome, and sent a force to stop Garibaldi. They met in battle and exchanged desultory fire. Garibaldi quickly forbade his men to fire on their fellow countrymen but was himself wounded in the foot and taken prisoner.

After a brief imprisonment, Garibaldi was allowed to return to Sardinia. But a quiet life eluded him. In 1866, he took up arms, this time with Victor Emmanuel's backing, to win Venetia, a region of northeastern Italy controlled by the Austrian Empire. After a few weeks of fighting, Austria handed Venetia over to the Kingdom of Italy, which also took control of Venice. Only the Papal States were needed to complete the unification of Italy. Garibaldi led a march on Rome, but was defeated by Papal–French forces and withdrew.

Italy went on to win back its ancient capital, but without any assistance from Garibaldi, and he, despite being a member of parliament, spent most of the rest of his life on his farm in Caprera.

1862
BLOOD AND IRON

OTTO VON BISMARCK
(1815–98)

Before the nineteenth century, Germany was divided into several states. Conservative statesman Otto von Bismarck was born in the powerful Kingdom of Prussia, which stretched from the Baltic to the Rhine. In 1815, the Treaty of Vienna had set up the German Confederation, a body that loosely tied the German-speaking states together, with the Austrian Empire as the senior partner. But Bismarck, along with his king and countrymen, believed Prussia should be in control.

In 1848, the German lands were swept up in a wave of revolutions across Europe – known as the March Revolution – aiming for unification. However, conflict between different political factions saw the Revolution fail. Bismarck was supportive of creating a united Germany, but only if Prussia was to be the dominant power.

In 1862, Prussia's liberal-controlled parliament refused to give King Wilhelm I funding for his plans to reform the army. Wilhelm I looked to Bismarck, a strongly conservative monarchist and proponent of military strength, to force them to reconsider. On 23 September, Bismarck was appointed to the offices of Prime Minister and Foreign Minister, making him the most powerful politician in Prussia. One week later, he made a speech to the Budget Committee that was withholding the funds.

—— THE SPEECH ——

. . . Furthermore, one is too sensitive about the government's mistakes; as if it were enough to say 'this and that cabinet minister made mistakes', as if one wasn't adversely affected oneself. Public opinion changes, the press is not the same as public opinion; one knows how the press is written. Members of parliament have a higher duty, to lead opinion, to stand above it. We are too hot-blooded, we have a preference for putting on armour that is too big for our small body; and now we're actually supposed to utilize it. Germany is not looking to Prussia's liberalism, but to its power; Bavaria, Württemberg, Baden may indulge liberalism, and for that reason no one will assign them Prussia's role; Prussia has to coalesce and concentrate its power for the opportune moment, which has already been missed several times; Prussia's borders according to the Vienna Treaties [of 1814–15] are not favourable for a healthy, vital state; it is not by speeches and majority resolutions that the great questions of the time are decided – that was the big mistake of 1848 and 1849 – but by iron and blood.

—— THE CONSEQUENCES——

Bismarck had argued that military force, or 'blood and iron', were more important than diplomacy or political debate. This adage was quickly proved in 1866, when Prussia declared war on Austria, and swiftly defeated her. The German Confederation was dissolved, and Austria was forced to promise never again to intervene in German affairs.

The following year, Prussia joined with Saxony and several other states to form the North German Federation, with Wilhelm I as its president and Bismarck its chancellor. Prussia's dominance unnerved the French. This suited Bismarck, who believed a war with France could unite all of Germany behind Prussia.

Bismarck, after several diplomatic provocations,

cleverly incited France into declaring war on Prussia on 19 July 1870. As he had predicted, the German lands rallied behind Prussia. In less than a month, the French armies were defeated and Paris was besieged. Sensing an opportunity, Bismarck quickly secured the support of the southern German states. On 18 January 1871, Wilhelm I was proclaimed Emperor, or Kaiser, of all Germany. Naturally, Bismarck was chosen as the first Imperial Chancellor. He had achieved his goal of unification.

1865
SECOND INAUGURAL ADDRESS

ABRAHAM LINCOLN

(1809–65)

In the mid-nineteenth century the question of slavery had split the United States. Abolition was favoured in the North, while slavery was vehemently supported in the South. In 1860, Lincoln, who had won national fame for his strong abolitionist views, was chosen as the presidential candidate of the recently created Republican Party, which had been founded to oppose slavery. He won the presidency, and assumed office in March 1861. In his inaugural address, Lincoln reached out to the South with the words 'we are not enemies, but friends'. It was to no avail. Eleven southern states seceded, forming the Confederate States of America, so they could continue to practise slavery.

Fighting began in April 1861. The ensuing conflict

was brutal. The turning point of the war came at the Battle of Gettysburg in 1863, when the North was victorious. In the founding ceremony of the cemetery for the casualties of Gettysburg, Lincoln delivered an address in which he vowed that 'these dead shall not have died in vain'. His promise was fulfilled. The Northern armies successfully advanced south.

On Lincoln's re-election as president in 1864, the war was virtually won. Yet when he delivered his second inaugural address, on 4 March 1865, Lincoln had another struggle in mind – the battle to reconstruct a nation ravaged by civil war.

—— THE SPEECH ——

. . . On the occasion corresponding to this four years ago, all thoughts were anxiously directed to an impending civil war. All dreaded it, all sought to avert it. While the inaugural address was being delivered from this place, devoted altogether to saving the Union without war, insurgent agents were in the city seeking to destroy it without war – seeking to dissolve the Union and divide effects by negotiation. Both parties deprecated war, but one of them would make war rather than let the nation survive, and the other would accept war rather than let it perish, and the war came.

One eighth of the whole population were colored

slaves, not distributed generally over the Union, but localized in the southern part of it. These slaves constituted a peculiar and powerful interest. All knew that this interest was somehow the cause of the war. To strengthen, perpetuate and extend this interest was the object for which the insurgents would rend the Union even by war, while the Government claimed no right to do more than to restrict the territorial enlargement of it. Neither party expected for the war the magnitude or the duration which it has already attained. Neither anticipated that the cause of the conflict might cease with or even before the conflict itself should cease. Each looked for an easier triumph, and a result less fundamental and astounding. Both read the same Bible and pray to the same God, and each invokes His aid against the other. It may seem strange that any men should dare to ask a just God's assistance in wringing their bread from the sweat of other men's faces, but let us judge not, that we be not judged. The prayers of both could not be answered. That of neither has been answered fully. The Almighty has His own purposes. 'Woe unto the world because of offenses; for it must needs be that offenses come, but woe to that man by whom the offense cometh.' If we shall suppose that American slavery is one of those offenses which, in the providence of God, must needs come, but which, having continued through His appointed time, He now wills to remove, and that He gives to both North and South this terrible war as the woe due to those by whom the offense came, shall we discern therein any departure from those divine attributes which the believers in a living God always ascribe to Him? Fondly do we hope, fervently do we pray, that this mighty scourge of war may speedily pass away. Yet, if God wills that it continue until all the wealth piled by the bondsman's two hundred and fifty years of unrequited toil shall be sunk, and until every drop of blood drawn with the lash shall be paid by another drawn with the sword, as was said three thousand years ago, so still it must be said 'the judgments of the Lord are true and righteous altogether'.

With malice toward none, with charity for all, with firmness in the right as God gives us to see the right, let us strive on to finish the work we are in, to bind up the nation's wounds, to care for him who shall have borne the battle and for his widow and his orphan, to do all which may achieve and cherish a just and lasting peace among ourselves and with all nations.

—— THE CONSEQUENCES ——

Lincoln's speech showed that he did not wish to see the South ravaged for its secession. He reminded his listeners that the consequences of war had been bloody and disastrous for both sides. Importantly, Lincoln's address reinforced his belief that the institution of slavery must be wholly eradicated. Official confirmation of the Northern victory came on 9 April 1865, when the Confederate general Robert E. Lee, leader of their main surviving army, surrendered. The Civil War had lasted for over four years, and had cost the lives of over half a million people.

Tragically, Lincoln would not live to oversee the recovery of the United States from war. In the crowds listening to his address had been John Wilkes Booth, a Confederate spy. On 14 April, he shot the president at a theatre and Lincoln died the next morning. Booth managed to flee from the scene but was eventually tracked down and killed later that month. Lincoln's Vice-President, Andrew Johnson, succeeded him. In December 1865, the Thirteenth Amendment, which constitutionally outlawed slavery, was passed. It is perhaps the finest legacy of Lincoln's remarkable life.

1915
IRELAND UNFREE SHALL
NEVER BE AT PEACE

PATRICK PEARSE

(1879–1916)

The Acts of Union 1800 merged Britain and
Ireland to form the United Kingdom of Great
Britain and Ireland. Not all Irishmen accepted British
rule, and there were numerous uprisings. From the
1870s, there were several failed attempts in Parliament
to enact legislation giving Ireland home rule, and it was
not until 1912 that such a bill was passed. Opponents
to home rule, based mainly in Northern Ireland,
formed the Ulster Volunteers. In response, supporters
of home rule established the Irish Volunteers. Patrick
Pearse, a poet, teacher and barrister, was one of their
first members.

The outbreak of World War I delayed the adoption of
the home-rule bill, which would ultimately never be

implemented. Nationalist groups, such as the Irish Republic Brotherhood, wanted outright independence from Britain and their own republic. Pearse joined the Brotherhood in 1913 and became one of its most important spokesmen and leaders. On 1 August 1915, he delivered a rousing graveside oration at the burial of Jeremiah O'Donovan Rossa in Dublin. O'Donovan Rossa had been a member of the Irish Republican Brotherhood since the 1850s, and his violent anti-British activities had led to imprisonment and eventual exile from Ireland to the United States. When he died in New York, his body was returned home for burial. Pearse addressed the crowds who had gathered for his funeral.

—— THE SPEECH ——

[...]

In a closer spiritual communion with him now than ever before, or perhaps ever again, in a spiritual communion with those of his day, living and dead, who suffered with him in English prisons, in communion of spirit too with our own dear comrades who suffer in English prisons today, and speaking on their behalf as well as our own, we pledge to Ireland our love, and we pledge to English rule in Ireland our hate. This is a place of peace, sacred to the dead, where men should speak with all charity and with all restraint; but I hold it a Christian thing, as O'Donovan Rossa held it, to hate evil, to hate untruth, to hate oppression, and, hating them, to strive to overthrow them. Our foes are strong and wise and wary; but, strong and wise and wary as they are, they cannot undo the miracles of God who ripens in the hearts of young men the seeds sown by the young men of a former generation. And the seeds sown by the young men of '65 and '67 are coming to their miraculous ripening today. Rulers and defenders of Realms had need to be wary if they would guard against such processes. Life springs from death; and from the graves of patriot men and women spring living nations. The defenders of this Realm have worked well in secret and in the open. They think that they have pacified Ireland. They think that they have purchased half of us and intimidated the other half. They think that they have foreseen everything, think that they have provided against everything, but the fools, the fools, the fools! They have left us with our Fenian dead, and while Ireland holds these graves, Ireland unfree shall never be at peace.

—— THE CONSEQUENCES ——

These words formed a prelude to an armed uprising with the aim of establishing an Irish Republic. The Irish

Republican Brotherhood, together with the Irish Volunteers, sought to take advantage of British preoccupation with fighting World War I. On Easter Monday 1916, the Irish rebels seized several key buildings in Dublin. From the steps of the General Post Office, Pearse proclaimed an independent Irish Republic, stating: 'We declare the right of the people in Ireland to the ownership of Ireland, and to the unfettered control of Irish destinies.'

The British troops rallied and fought back to retain control of Dublin. Hundreds of civilians died in the fighting and British shelling damaged many buildings. Uprisings elsewhere in Ireland had not been very successful. After six days, the rebel position in Dublin was untenable. To prevent further violence, Pearse surrendered to the British and was imprisoned along with other rebel leaders. He was killed by firing squad on 3 May.

In the aftermath of the Easter Rising, the surviving nationalist supporters joined the Sinn Féin Party (from the Gaelic for 'we ourselves'). Largely owing to Britain's actions during the Easter Rising, the separatist party went on to win the majority of seats in the 1918 election.

An end of strife

In 1920, a new home-rule bill split Ireland in two, with each part to have its own parliament but remain part of the United Kingdom. Sinn Féin rejected partition, demanding full independence of all Ireland. The fighting between the Irish Republican Army and British forces continued, with atrocities on both sides. King George V (1865–1936) offered to travel to Belfast to open the new Northern Ireland Parliament – a brave decision as violence was endemic in the city. In his speech, George appealed for an end to bloodshed: 'I pray that my coming to Ireland today may prove to be the first step towards an end of strife amongst her people, whatever their race or creed. 'He appealed to all Irishmen to join in, making for the land which they love a new era of peace, contentment and good will.

A truce was declared on 9 July, and negotiations began. The Anglo-Irish Treaty was signed in December, creating an Irish Free State. Importantly, it gave Northern Ireland the option of withdrawing from the new nation, which it did. In June 1922, civil war broke out in the Irish Free State between the supporters and opponents of partition. After ten months of fighting, the supporters were victorious: Ireland was independent but separated.

1915
ADDRESS BEFORE THE
DEFENCE OF BELGRADE

DRAGUTIN GAVRILOVIĆ
(1882–1945)

In 1914, Europe's major forces were arrayed against each other in two power blocs; the Triple Entente of Russia, France and Britain, and the Triple Alliance of Germany, Austria-Hungary and Turkey. The catalyst for war was in the Balkan region, the 'powder keg of Europe'. Both major powers and local nations vied for control. In Serbia, there was a desire to unite all of the Southern Slavic lands. To that end, the nation had designs on the province of Bosnia-Herzegovina, which Austria-Hungary had recently annexed.

On 28 June 1914, Archduke Franz Ferdinand, the heir to the Austro-Hungarian throne, was assassinated while visiting Sarajevo by Gavrilo Princep, a member of the revolutionary Young Bosnia movement, which had close ties with Serbia. Austria-Hungary used this as a pretext for declaring war on Serbia. Immediately, Russia began to mobilize its armies to protect its Serbian ally, while Germany, facing a potential war on two fronts, marched on France – aiming to swiftly defeat her before Russia could fully mobilize. The British were forced to declare war on Germany.

As Austria-Hungary crossed the border into Serbia, hoping to knock them out of the war as soon as possible, Dragutin Gavrilović, a major in the Serb army, successfully helped lead the defence, forcing a retreat.

On 7 October 1915, the Austro-Hungarians advanced into Serbia again, this time with German support. Gavrilović was leading a unit charged with protecting the capital, Belgrade. The unit bravely fought back wave after wave of Austro-Hungarian attack. As the day wore on, and on the point of defeat, Gavrilović addressed his men.

—— THE SPEECH ——

Soldiers! At three o'clock sharp, the enemy is to be defeated with your forceful attack, destroyed with your bombs and bayonets. The honour of Belgrade, our capital, has to be saved. Soldiers! Heroes! Supreme command has deleted our regiment from the list. Our regiment has been sacrificed for the honour of

Belgrade and the Homeland. You should not worry for your lives as they do not exist any more. So, let's go forward towards glory! For King and Homeland! Long live the King! Long live Belgrade!

— THE CONSEQUENCES —

Gavrilović then personally led a charge, attempting to force the Austro-Hungarians back. He was wounded in the fighting. The Serbs were unable to prevent the Austro-Hungarians from advancing into Belgrade. After two days of bitter combat in the city, sometimes hand-to-hand, Belgrade fell. To make matters worse, neighbouring Bulgaria launched an invasion of Serbia. The country now lay in enemy hands. King Peter I of Serbia was forced to lead his army in a retreat south towards Greece. The soldiers suffered from cold, hunger and disease during their long march, and many died.

In September 1918, the Serbs, and their allies, launched a massed offensive to recapture their homeland. Two weeks before World War I ended, Serbia was liberated. After the war, Austria-Hungary was dismantled. Their provinces in the Balkans were joined with Serbia and Montenegro to create a new nation, renamed Yugoslavia in 1929. Gavrilović survived the war, and won numerous awards for heroism and valour.

1916
APPEAL FOR NATIONAL SERVICE

ROBERT LAIRD BORDEN

(1854-1937)

In 1914, Canada was a dominion of the British Empire; it was self-governing but had no control over foreign policy. Therefore, when Britain declared war on Germany on 4 August, Canada was at war as well. Its prime minister, Robert Laird Borden, was a supporter of the war and pledged to send half a million men to fight. For a country of under eight million, this was a huge number. Thousands of Canadians answered Britain's call, very few of whom came from Québec, where the mostly French-speaking population resented serving British interests.

The Battle of the Somme began in July 1916. Twenty-five thousand troops from Canada died in the fighting, which saw horrific casualties on all sides. As it stood, volunteers alone were not sufficient to meet Borden's commitment to Britain. Reluctant to introduce conscription, on 23 October, Borden made a speech exhorting more Canadians to volunteer – despite the fact that 370,000 men had already enlisted and 285,000 had been sent overseas.

—— THE SPEECH ——

To the People of Canada: the worldwide struggle in which our Empire is fighting for its rights, its liberties and its very existence has continued for more than two years. Every effort that could honourably be made on our part to avert war was put forth with the deepest earnestness and sincerity. There was no escape from the contest save in dishonour and ultimate disaster. The wonderful extent and thoroughness of the enemy's long and careful preparation was imperfectly understood at first, and the magnitude of the struggle has surpassed all anticipation. Great Britain's first expeditionary force has been increased more than twentyfold, and that of Canada more than twelvefold. The climax of the war is rapidly approaching. The last hundred thousand men that Canada will place in the fighting line may be the deciding factor in a struggle the issue of which will determine the destiny of this Dominion, of our Empire, and of the whole world.

The most eloquent tribute would fail to do fitting honour to the youth of Canada who have already rallied so splendidly to the colours and whose heroic valour and glorious achievements have crowned this Dominion with imperishable distinction before the world. Remembering the sacrifice by which that distinction was won, we recall with solemn pride the undying memory of those who had fallen.

In the history of every people there may come such a challenge to the spirit of its citizens as must be answered in service and devotion if the nation is to have an abiding peace in the future. The events of this war bring that challenge today to the manhood of Canada.

[. . .]

Let us never forget the solemn truth that the nation is not constituted of the living alone. There are those as well who have passed away and those yet to be born. So this great responsibility comes to us as heirs of the past and trustees of the future. But with that responsibility there has come something greater still, the opportunity of proving ourselves worthy of it; and I pray that this may not be lost.

And still there were insufficient Canadian volunteers. Therefore, in August 1917, Borden's government passed the Military Service Act, which introduced controversial conscription. To hold together the government, Borden recruited some opposition members of parliament to form a new party, the Unionists. They won the 1917 elections. Borden continued as prime minister. In 1918, protests broke out against conscription in Québec. Government offices were attacked and Borden sent in soldiers to keep the peace. That Easter, violent riots broke out in the city. Government forces fired on the crowds, killing some and wounding many more.

While conscription raised 120,000 soldiers, only around one-quarter of them actually reached the front. By the time the war ended in 1918, over 600,000 Canadians had served in the armed forces, and 60,000 had died. During the peace talks in Paris, Borden insisted that Canada have its own voice. He retired from office in 1920, but his post-war actions paved the way for complete Canadian independence in 1931.

Canada continued to be part of the Commonwealth and, in 1939, would follow Britain in declaring war on Nazi Germany, this time as a fully independent nation. Over one million Canadians served in World War II.

1917
GERMANY EXPECTED TO FIND A LAMB AND FOUND A LION

DAVID LLOYD GEORGE
(1863–1945)

The 1839 Treaty of London obliged Britain to come to Belgium's aide if any power invaded. With World War I looming, Germany's strategy, the Schlieffen Plan, relied on invading the Low Countries, advancing through Belgium, before defeating France. The Germans did not believe the British would honour the treaty and, on 3 August, they advanced into Belgium. The next day, Britain declared war on Germany.

In 1915, Prime Minister H. H. Asquith formed a coalition government with the Conservatives after a scandal over a shortage of shells on the front. David Lloyd George, one of the most influential politicians in Europe, successfully worked to ensure the British army would not face any more shortages in munitions. He grew frustrated with Asquith, who he did not feel was an effective war leader. In December 1916, Asquith was forced out of office. Splitting the Liberal Party, Lloyd George became Prime Minister with Conservative support, providing Britain with more dynamic leadership. On 21 June 1917, he made a speech to Parliament, blaming German aggression for the war.

—— THE SPEECH ——

It is a satisfaction for Britain in these terrible times that no share of the responsibility for these events rests on her. She is not the Jonah in this storm. The part taken by our country in this conflict, in its origin, and in its conduct, has been as honourable and chivalrous as any part ever taken in any country in any operation.

[. . .]

What are the main facts? There were six countries which entered the war at the beginning. Britain was last, and not the first. Before she entered the war, Britain made every effort to avoid it; begged, supplicated and entreated that there should be no conflict. I was a member of the Cabinet at the time, and I remember the earnest endeavours we made to persuade Germany and Austria not to precipitate Europe into this welter of blood. We begged them to summon a European conference to consider. Had that conference met, arguments against provoking such a catastrophe were so overwhelming that there would never have been a war. Germany knew that, so she rejected the conference, although Austria was prepared to accept it. She suddenly declared war, and yet we are the people who wantonly provoked this war, in order to attack Germany. We begged Germany not to attack Belgium, and produced a treaty, signed by the King of Prussia, as well as the King of England, pledging himself to protect Belgium against an invader, and we said, 'If you invade Belgium, we shall have no alternative but to defend it.' The enemy invaded Belgium, and now they say, 'Why, forsooth, you, England, provoked this war.' It is not quite the story of the wolf and the lamb. I will tell you why – because Germany expected to find a lamb and found a lion.

—— THE CONSEQUENCES——

Lloyd George led Britain for the rest of the war. One of his most important acts was to introduce a convoy system to protect British shipping, preventing the German submarine campaign from starving Britain into submission. Victory over the Germans arrived in

1918. One month after the war ended, Lloyd George won a landslide victory leading a coalition of Conservatives and Liberal supporters. He wanted to ensure veterans would return to 'homes fit for heroes', and instituted government funding for new housing.

In 1922, Lloyd George was caught up in a scandal over the sale of knighthoods and peerages. The Conservatives left the coalition and he stood down as Prime Minister. He managed to reunite the Liberals but could only lead them to a crushing defeat in the 1924 general election.

Lloyd George would be Britain's final Liberal Prime Minister. He remained a member of parliament until 1945, but did not live to see Britain decisively win World War II, dying on 26 March the same year.

1917
AN APPEAL TO THE RED ARMY

VLADIMIR LENIN
(1870–1924)

Born Vladimir Ilyich Ulyanov, Lenin was involved in socialist revolutionary circles from a young age. His activities caught the eye of the authorities and he was arrested in 1895 and exiled to Siberia.

Lenin returned to Russia in 1905, when protests against Tsar Nicholas II's absolute rule swept the country. Nicholas remained in control and Lenin returned to Western Europe. When World War I broke out in 1914, Russia initially rallied behind Nicholas but support waned and, in March 1917, there were mass demonstrations against the war, which resulted in Nicholas's abdication.

Lenin, living in Switzerland, was desperate to return to Russia. The Germans, hoping his revolutionary activities would disrupt the Russian war effort, gave him permission to travel through their lands in a sealed train to neutral Sweden, and then on to Russia.

In November, Lenin's Bolsheviks overthrew the Provisional Government with the support of the Soviets. Lenin established a communist government and under his rule, Russia made peace with the Germans. A new military force, the Red Army, was created to defend the revolution, while opposition groups coalesced to form the White Army, with the support of foreign powers who distrusted the Bolsheviks. The ensuing Russian Civil War was a bitter and damaging conflict, during which Lenin instituted a system of 'War Communism'. Industry was nationalized and workers faced strict discipline and compulsory labour. The Whites advanced towards the heart of Communist power in Central Russia. On 29 March 1919, Lenin made a speech to the Red Army, appealing to them to continue their struggle.

—— THE SPEECH ——

Comrades, Red Army men! The capitalists of Britain, America and France are waging war against Russia. They are taking revenge on the Soviet workers' and peasants' republic for having overthrown the power of the landowners and capitalists and thereby set an example to all the nations of the globe. The capitalists of Britain, France and America are helping with money and munitions the Russian landowners who are bringing troops from Siberia, the Don and North Caucasus against Soviet power for the purpose of restoring the rule of the tsar and the power of the landowners and capitalists. But this will not happen. The Red Army has closed its ranks, has risen up and driven the landowners' troops and whiteguard officers from the Volga, has recaptured Riga and almost the whole of the Ukraine, and is marching towards Odessa and Rostov. A little more effort, a few more months of fighting the enemy, and victory will be ours. The Red Army is strong because it is consciously and unitedly marching into battle for the peasants' land, for the rule of the workers and peasants, for Soviet power.

The Red Army is invincible because it has united millions of working peasants with the workers who have now learned to fight, have acquired comradely discipline, who do not lose heart, who become steeled after slight reverses, and are more and more boldly marching against the enemy, convinced he will soon be defeated.

[. . .]

Comrades, Red Army men! Be staunch, firm and united. March boldly forward against the enemy.

Victory will be ours. The power of the landowners and the capitalists, broken in Russia, will be defeated throughout the world.

—— THE CONSEQUENCES ——

The Communists fought back against the Whites. Lenin's revolutionary comrade Leon Trotsky reformed the Red Army, establishing strict discipline. Deserters were shot, and soldiers were stationed behind unreliable units to ensure they would not flee from battle. In addition to the chaos of civil war, Russia faced a devastating famine in 1921, which killed millions.

The Whites were finally defeated in 1922. War had devastated the country but Lenin had established Communist control of Russia and its neighbouring lands. The new territory was called the Union of Soviet Socialist Republics. Lenin would not live long to rule over the state he had forged; he suffered a series of strokes, the last of which left him mute and bedridden. Lenin was forced to retire from the leadership of the Soviet Union, and died on 21 January 1924 in his estate near Moscow. A 'troika' of three politicians replaced him, one of whom was Stalin. He would go on to become the de facto leader for almost thirty years.

1917
WAR MESSAGE TO CONGRESS

WOODROW WILSON

(1856–1924)

Woodrow Wilson was President of the United States when World War I broke out in 1914. He endeavoured to keep the United States neutral and offered to broker a peace deal between the two sides, but the combatants were not interested in negotiations. American public opinion grew increasingly anti-German, fuelled by lurid accounts of alleged German atrocities in Belgium.

In 1915, Germany declared the waters around the British Isles a war zone, using their submarines to attack ships. On 7 May, a German submarine sunk the ocean liner *Lusitania*, killing over one thousand people, including 128 Americans. Wilson protested Germany's policy, but still did not enter the war.

In 1916, Wilson won a second term as president, campaigning under the slogan, 'He kept us out of the war'. This claim was short-lived. In 1917, Germany stepped up their submarine attacks, causing hundreds of civilian deaths. The final straw was the Zimmermann Telegram – a message from Germany to Mexico proposing an alliance if the United States entered the war. Mexico would reject the offer but the British intercepted the telegram, and passed it on to the Americans. It was clear to Wilson that entering the war was necessary. On 2 April, he informed Congress of his decision.

—— THE SPEECH ——

. . . The world must be made safe for democracy. Its peace must be planted upon the tested foundations of political liberty. We have no selfish ends to serve. We desire no conquest, no dominion. We seek no indemnities for ourselves, no material compensation for the sacrifices we shall freely make. We are but one of the champions of the rights of mankind. We shall be satisfied when those rights have been made as secure as the faith and the freedom of nations can make them.

[. . .]

There are, it may be, many months of fiery trial and

sacrifice ahead of us. It is a fearful thing to lead this great peaceful people into war, into the most terrible and disastrous of all wars, civilization itself seeming to be in the balance. But the right is more precious than peace, and we shall fight for the things which we have always carried nearest our hearts – for democracy, for the right of those who submit to authority to have a voice in their own governments, for the rights and liberties of small nations, for a universal dominion of right by such a concert of free peoples as shall bring peace and safety to all nations and make the world itself at last free. To such a task we can dedicate our lives and our fortunes, everything that we are and everything that we have, with the pride of those who know that the day has come when America is privileged to spend her blood and her might for the principles that gave her birth and happiness and the peace which she has treasured. God helping her, she can do no other.

—— THE CONSEQUENCES ——

Congress voted in favour of entering the war. The United States declared war on Germany on 6 April. Conscription was introduced and an expeditionary force sent to Europe. American troops played an important role in pushing the Germans back. In November, Germany agreed to end the fighting.

In 1919, Wilson travelled to Paris to take part in the peace talks, hoping to promote his ambitious plans for a post-war world (the 'Fourteen Points', which included plans for a reduction in arms and the creation of an international association of nations). Wilson's ideals were of little interest to his allies, although the establishment of his League of Nations was included in the Treaty of Versailles and Wilson was awarded the Nobel Peace Prize for his efforts.

Tragically, when Wilson returned home, he was unable to win support for American entry into the League of Nations, and, in October 1919, Wilson suffered from a major stroke, which left him unable to take an active role in government. After his term as president ended, Wilson retired from public life and died on 3 February 1924. His message that the United States should intervene abroad to promote democracy would become a major part of American foreign policy, and have a profound bearing on world history.

1936
APPEAL TO THE LEAGUE
OF NATIONS

EMPEROR HAILE SELASSIE I
(1892–1975)

In the late nineteenth century, European powers scrambled to carve up and colonize Africa. Remaining independent was the Ethiopian Empire, which had roundly defeated Italy's attempted conquest in 1895–6. In 1916, Zewditu became Ethiopia's first empress. Her nephew was chosen as her heir and regent. His name was Tafari Makonnen, but he would be better known by his coronation name, Haile Selassie (which means 'Power of the Trinity'). He aimed to reform Ethiopia and was instrumental in its admittance to the League of Nations in 1923. Haile Selassie became emperor on Zewditu's death in 1930.

Meanwhile, Benito Mussolini had risen to power in Italy and wanted to add to his nation's existing possessions in East Africa by conquering Ethiopia. The Italians advanced into Ethiopia in October 1935. The League of Nations, of which both states were members, did nothing to come to Ethiopia's aid. Despite Italy's modern air force and use of chemical warfare, the Ethiopians successfully fought back, with Haile Selassie sometimes personally commanding his armies.

By spring 1936, the Italians had begun to push forward towards Ethiopia's capital, Addis Ababa. With the situation desperate, Haile Selassie departed for Geneva to personally appeal to the League of Nations. By the time he addressed the League on 30 June, Mussolini had declared Ethiopia to be an Italian province.

—— THE SPEECH ——

I, Haile Selassie I, Emperor of Ethiopia, am here today to claim that justice which is due to my people, and the assistance promised to it eight months ago, when fifty nations asserted that aggression had been committed in violation of international treaties. There is no precedent for a Head of State himself speaking in this assembly. But there is also no precedent for a people being victim of such injustice and being at present threatened by abandonment to its aggressor. Also, there has never before been an example of any Government proceeding to the systematic extermination of a nation by barbarous means, in violation of the most solemn promises made by the nations of the earth that there should not be used against innocent human beings the terrible poison of harmful gases. It is to defend a people struggling for its age-old independence that the head of the Ethiopian Empire has come to Geneva to fulfill this supreme duty, after having himself fought at the head of his armies.

[. . .]

Apart from the Kingdom of the Lord there is not on this earth any nation that is superior to any other. Should it happen that a strong Government finds it may with impunity destroy a weak people, then the hour strikes for that weak people to appeal to the League of Nations to give its judgement in all freedom. God and history will remember your judgement.

[. . .]

I ask the fifty-two nations, who have given the Ethiopian people a promise to help them in their resistance to the aggressor, what are they willing to do for Ethiopia? And the great Powers who have promised the guarantee of collective security to small States on whom weighs the threat that they may one day suffer the fate of Ethiopia, I ask what measures do you intend to take? Representatives of the World, I have come to Geneva to discharge in your midst the most painful of the duties of the head of a State. What reply shall I have to take back to my people?

—— THE CONSEQUENCES ——

Haile Selassie was unable to take back any reply to his people. The League did nothing. Haile Selassie moved to England, where he continued to speak out against the occupation of Ethiopia, but it was not until the outbreak of World War II that anything was accomplished. In 1941, he re-entered Ethiopia along with an Allied army, and defeated the Italians. Ethiopia became the first nation to be liberated from the Axis powers, and Haile Selassie was restored as emperor.

After the war ended, Ethiopia became a charter member of the United Nations. In 1963, Haile Selassie helped to found the Organization of African Unity, which had its headquarters in Addis Ababa. He was its first chair. By the 1970s, however, Haile Selassie's authority began to erode. There was student and peasant unrest, as well as outbreaks of famine. In 1974, riots broke out in the capital. The Derg, a Soviet-backed army committee, deposed Haile Selassie and seized power. Ethiopia's last emperor, and defender of its independence, died under house arrest the following year.

The invasion of Ethiopia

Benito Mussolini (1883–1945) wanted to carve out a new Roman Empire – 'a place in the sun', as he termed it. On 2 October 1935, one day before his troops invaded Ethiopia, Mussolini addressed Italy, 'the wheels of destiny have been moving toward their goal . . . their rhythm has become more swift and by now cannot be stopped'. He brushed aside fear of reprisals from other nations and warned:, 'let no one think that he can make us yield without a hard struggle'. He called upon the Italian people to 'let the cry of your decision fill the heavens . . . a warning to enemies in every part of the world'.

His conquest of Ethiopia attracted some criticism but Italy faced no significant sanctions, despite their use of poison gas. Mussolini's decision to involve Italy in World War II proved his downfall. In 1943, the Allies landed in Sicily and advanced north. Mussolini managed to hold on to power in the northernmost areas of the country with Nazi support, but he became little more than a puppet ruler. In 1945, communist partisans captured him and his mistress while they were trying to flee Italy. They were both shot. Mussolini's body was then strung up in public and subjected to the depredations of the public.

1938
FAREWELL TO
THE INTERNATIONAL
BRIGADES

D O L O R E S   I B Á R R U R I ,
' L A   P A S I O N A R I A '
(1 8 9 5 – 1 9 8 9)

In the 1930s, Spain was divided into warring
factions: Nationalist and Republican. Both sides
looked abroad for help. The Nationalists, led by
General Francisco Franco, received help from fascist
Germany and Italy, who sent men, money and
equipment. The Republicans were backed (to a lesser
degree) by Mexico and the Soviet Union. Their most
famous foreign supporters were the International
Brigades. Foreigners also served in Spanish battalions –
the English writer George Orwell fought for the
Workers' Party of Marxist Unification – and over the
course of the war, around 40,000 people fought for
the Republic.

The Republican forces and the International

Brigades were called into action when Franco launched an assault on the Republican capital, Madrid, in November 1936. Dolores Ibárruri, a communist activist and politician known as 'La Pasionaria' ('The Passionflower') who had achieved renown for her fiery speeches, rallied the Republican troops with her declaration of ¡No Pasarán! ('They shall not pass!'), and the Nationalists were unable to capture Madrid.

As the Spanish Civil War continued, conflict among different political factions wrecked the Republican war effort. In May 1937, Communist and Anarchist groups fought openly in the streets of Barcelona. Franco pressed on, taking control of all Northern Spain by the end of 1937.

In October 1938, the League of Nations ordered the withdrawal of the International Brigades (ignoring the foreigners fighting for the Nationalists). The Republican government complied with the demand, wrongly hoping it would end the international embargo on the sale of weapons. On 1 November, Ibárruri said goodbye to the foreign volunteers in Barcelona.

—— THE SPEECH——

It is very difficult to say a few words in farewell to the heroes of the International Brigades, because of what they are and what they represent. A feeling of sorrow, an infinite grief catches our throat – sorrow for those who are going away, for the soldiers of the highest ideal of human redemption, exiles from their countries, persecuted by the tyrants of all peoples – grief for those who will stay here forever mingled with the Spanish soil, in the very depth of our heart, hallowed by our feeling of eternal gratitude.

From all peoples, from all races, you came to us like brothers, like sons of immortal Spain; and in the hardest days of the war, when the capital of the Spanish Republic was threatened, it was you, gallant comrades of the International Brigades, who helped save the city with your fighting enthusiasm, your heroism and your spirit of sacrifice.

[. . .]

Communists, Socialists, Anarchists, Republicans – men of different colours, differing ideology, antagonistic religions – yet all profoundly loving liberty and justice, they came and offered themselves to us unconditionally. They gave us everything – their youth or their maturity; their science or their experience; their blood and their lives; their hopes and aspirations – and they asked us for nothing. But yes, it must be said, they did want a post in battle, they aspired to the honour of dying for us.

[. . .]

Coming over seas and mountains, crossing frontiers bristling with bayonets, sought by raving dogs thirsting to tear their flesh, these men reached our country as crusaders for freedom, to fight and die for Spain's liberty and independence threatened by German and Italian fascism. They gave up everything – their loves, their countries, home and fortune, fathers, mothers, wives, brothers, sisters and children – and they came and said to us: 'We are here. Your cause, Spain's cause, is ours. It is the cause of all advanced and progressive mankind.'

—— THE CONSEQUENCES ——

The Republicans, increasingly beset by political in-fighting, continued to lose ground to the Nationalists. Barcelona fell in January 1939. In March, Ibárruri and the rest of the Republican leadership fled Spain and their forces began to disintegrate. The Nationalists entered Madrid and Franco proclaimed victory, becoming Spain's dictator. Around half a million people died in the fighting.

Ibárruri eventually settled in the Soviet Union. Her son died fighting the Germans at the Battle of Stalingrad in 1942. She returned home in 1977, after

Franco's death. Elections were held that June. Ibárruri's Communist Party won around ten per cent of the vote, and she was elected to Spain's new legislative body, stepping down before the 1979 elections. Despite an attempted military coup in 1981, Spain emerged as a democracy.

1939
REICHSTAG SPEECH

ADOLF HITLER
(1889–1945)

Adolf Hitler's gift as an orator was central to his rise to power in the political sphere, and marked him out as a natural leader. He became chancellor in 1933 and president in 1934. Now the unchallenged leader of Germany, all soldiers were made to swear a personal oath of loyalty to him. Hitler was determined to reverse the terms of the Treaty of Versailles, which had imposed severe economic sanctions, and to bring together all the German-speaking peoples, winning them living space (*Lebensraum*) in the East. Germany marched troops into the Rhineland, unified with Austria, successfully invaded Czechoslovakia, and built up its armies.

Hitler's next target was Poland. Although Britain and

France had guaranteed Polish independence, Hitler did not believe they would move against him. In preparation for the invasion, Germany signed a non-aggression pact with the Soviet Union (the Molotov-Ribbentrop Pact), which included secret plans to partition Poland. To create a *casus belli* and allow Hitler to claim he was acting in self-defense, German forces pretending to be Poles attacked a German radio tower on 31 August 1939. Early the next morning, the Luftwaffe launched raids in Poland and the German army began to march into Polish territory. That day, Hitler addressed the Reichstag.

—— THE SPEECH ——

This night for the first time Polish regular soldiers fired on our territory. Since 5.45 a.m. we have been returning the fire, and from now on bombs will be met by bombs. Whoever fight with poison gas will be fought with poison gas. Whoever departs from the rules of humane warfare can only expect that we shall do the same. I will continue this struggle, no matter against whom, until the safety of the Reich and its rights are secured.

[. . .]

I am asking of no German man more than I myself was ready throughout four years at any time to do. There will be no hardships for Germans to which I myself will not submit. My whole life henceforth belongs more than ever to my people. I am from now on just first soldier of the German Reich. I have once more put on that coat that was the most sacred and dear to me. I will not take it off again until victory is secured, or I will not survive the outcome.

[. . .]

As a National Socialist and as a German soldier I enter upon this struggle with a stout heart. My whole life has been nothing but one long struggle for my people, for its restoration, and for Germany. There was only one watchword for that struggle: faith in this people. One word I have never learned: that is, surrender.

[. . .]

Whoever, however, thinks he can oppose this national command, whether directly or indirectly, shall fall. We have nothing to do with traitors. We are all faithful to our old principle. It is quite unimportant whether we ourselves live, but it is essential that our people shall live, that Germany shall live. The sacrifice that is demanded of us is not greater than the sacrifice that many generations have made. If we form a community closely bound together by vows, ready for anything, resolved never to surrender, then our will will master every hardship and difficulty. And I would like to close with the declaration that I once made when I began the struggle for power in the Reich. I then said: 'If our will is so strong that no hardship and suffering can subdue it, then our will and our German might shall prevail.'

—— THE CONSEQUENCES ——

Hitler's claims that Poland had provoked the invasion were entirely fatuous. In response to his invasion, Britain and France declared war on Germany on 3 September. The Allies' decision to finally take a stand against Hitler came too late for Poland. Germany's armies swept away determined Polish resistance and advanced steadily, while the Soviets invaded Poland from the east. By October, the independent nation of Poland had been carved up and erased from the map. German success continued in Denmark and Norway; the Low Countries quickly followed and, in June, France surrendered. Hitler dominated Europe, with only Britain standing against him in the continent.

In 1941, Hitler invaded the Soviet Union and, the same year, he also declared war on the United States after his Japanses allies attacked Pearl Harbor. With

Hitler's approval, the Nazis set about the systematic extermination of Europe's Jewish population. Six million Jews were killed along with millions of other people the Nazis deemed 'undesirable'.

From 1942, the tide of the war gradually began to turn. After the D–Day landings, the Allies advanced on Germany from the east and west. Many believed Hitler was leading Germany to disaster. Indeed, by April 1945, the war was all but lost. Hitler was isolated in his bunker in Berlin, with Allied armies converging on him. On 29 April, Hitler married his long-term mistress, Eva Braun. The next day, they both committed suicide. Germany finally surrendered to the Allies on 8 May. Hitler's legacy was a devastated and ravaged continent, and a conflict that had killed millions, soldier and civilian alike.

1940
WE SHALL FIGHT ON THE BEACHES

WINSTON CHURCHILL

(1874–1965)

When Hitler invaded Poland in September 1939, the British Prime Minister Neville Chamberlain could no longer appease the Nazi leader. France and Britain declared war on Germany. The most outspoken critic of appeasement was Winston Churchill, who had previously played a major role in government during World War I. As a result of his opposition to Hitler, Churchill was invited to join Chamberlain's War Cabinet.

In April 1940, the Germans launched a successful invasion of Norway, without serious opposition from the Allies. The failure seriously damaged Chamberlain's prestige, and he was forced to resign on 10 May. Churchill was appointed Prime Minister.

Hours after the political upheaval, Hitler launched a

sudden invasion of France through the Low Countries. The Allied armies were powerless to stop the Nazi advance and were forced back to the port of Dunkirk. Churchill had no choice but to authorize their evacuation. The Germans were unable to break through to Dunkirk until 4 June. By then, 338,226 troops had been successfully evacuated. That day, Churchill addressed Parliament about the future of the war, and the possibility of invasion.

—— THE SPEECH ——

. . . Turning once again, and this time more generally, to the question of invasion, I would observe that there has never been a period in all these long centuries of which we boast when an absolute guarantee against invasion, still less against serious raids, could have been given to our people. In the days of Napoleon, the same wind which would have carried his transports across the Channel might have driven away the blockading fleet. There was always the chance, and it is that chance which has excited and befooled the imaginations of many Continental tyrants. Many are the tales that are told. We are assured that novel methods will be adopted, and when we see the originality of malice, the ingenuity of aggression, which our enemy displays, we may certainly prepare ourselves for every kind of novel stratagem and every kind of brutal and treacherous manoeuvre. I think that no idea is so outlandish that it should not be considered and viewed with a searching, but at the same time, I hope, with a steady eye. We must never forget the solid assurances of sea power and those which belong to air power if it can be locally exercised.

I have, myself, full confidence that if all do their duty, if nothing is neglected, and if the best arrangements are made, as they are being made, we shall prove ourselves once again able to defend our Island home, to ride out the storm of war, and to outlive the menace of tyranny, if necessary for years, if necessary alone. At any rate, that is what we are going to try to do. That is the resolve of His Majesty's Government – every man of them. That is the will of Parliament and the nation. The British Empire and the French Republic, linked together in their cause and in their need, will defend to the death their native soil, aiding each other like good comrades to the utmost of their strength. Even though large tracts of Europe and many old and famous States have fallen or may fall into the grip of the Gestapo and all the odious apparatus of Nazi rule, we shall not flag or fail. We shall go on to the end, we shall fight in France, we shall fight on the seas and oceans, we shall fight with growing confidence and growing strength in the air, we shall defend our Island, whatever the cost may be, we shall fight on the beaches, we shall fight on the landing grounds, we shall fight in the fields and in the streets, we shall fight in the hills; we shall never surrender, and even if, which I do not for a moment believe, this Island or a large part of it were subjugated and starving, then our Empire beyond the seas, armed and guarded by the British Fleet, would carry on the struggle, until, in God's good time, the New World, with all its power and might, steps forth to the rescue and the liberation of the old.

——THE CONSEQUENCES——

Churchill's stirring words were matched by his inspirational leadership. Britain stood alone in Europe against Hitler. France and Germany made peace in June. Germany turned its attention to invading Britain. The first step was for the Germans to gain aerial superiority over southern England. Galvanized by Churchill's leadership, the Royal Air Force fought off the Germans. Churchill paid tribute to the airmen, stating: 'Never was so much owed by so many to so few.'

With plans to invade postponed, Germany began a bombing campaign of civilian targets. Britain was battered but stood firm. The war turned in 1941. That June, the Soviet Union entered the war after Hitler launched a surprise invasion. The United States followed in December. Churchill negotiated the difficult progress of forming a successful alliance with the ideologically disparate figures of Josef Stalin and Franklin D. Roosevelt. In 1945, Germany and Japan were defeated. Not seen as a peacetime leader, Churchill lost the 1945 election to Clement Atlee. He won re-election in 1951, but stood down as Prime Minister four years later. Churchill, the most iconic of leaders and one of the most important figures in British history, died after a severe stroke in 1965.

Where She Goes, We Go

The New Zealand government declared war on Nazi Germany on the same day as Britain. As in World War I, in which around 100,000 Kiwis had served, New Zealand vowed to follow the 'Home Country'. Michael Joseph Savage (1872–1940), the country's first Labour leader and founder of its welfare state, had led the country since 1935, and had strongly opposed the appeasement of Adolf Hitler. When war broke out, Savage was battling colon cancer, but addressed the nation from his sickbed in a radio broadcast on 5 September. He encouraged the listening public to rally behind Britain: 'Where she stands, we stand. We are only a small and young nation, but we are one and all a band of brothers and we march forward with union of hearts and wills to a common destiny.'

The other Commonwealth nations had all followed Britain's declaration of war, and their men and support were vital to the Allied war effort. Around 140,000 New Zealanders served overseas during World War II, fighting in Europe, North Africa and the Pacific. Savage died of his illness on 27 March 1940, and is generally regarded as New Zealand's greatest prime minister.

1940
THE FLAME OF FRENCH RESISTANCE

CHARLES DE GAULLE
(1890–1970)

C harles de Gaulle served as an officer in World War I, and had spent two years in Germany as a prisoner of war. When the fighting ended, de Gaulle continued to serve in the army but his bold ideas for reform made him unpopular and, when World War II broke out, he was still just a colonel.

In May 1940, the Germans invaded France. They were equipped with fully integrated tanks, infantry, artillery and air support, and formed a cohesive fighting machine. By comparison, the French army, though larger, seemed positively antiquated. De Gaulle, in command of a tank regiment, was one of the few leaders successful in driving back the Germans, and won promotion to brigadier-general; but such successes were rare.

The Germans won the Low Countries, overwhelmed the French defences of the Maginot Line, and forced the evacuation of the British at Dunkirk. On 14 June, Paris fell. Two days later, the prime minister resigned. De Gaulle, unlike many in the army and government, was stridently opposed to any notion of surrender, while France's new leader, Philippe Pétain (who had been commander-in-chief of the French army during World War I), believed France's position was untenable and wanted to make peace with Germany. When de Gaulle heard of these plans, he fled to London to carry on the fight against Germany from exile. On 18 June, he addressed the people of France on the BBC.

—— THE SPEECH ——

. . . Speaking in full knowledge of the facts, I ask you to believe me when I say that the cause of France is not lost. The very factors that brought about our defeat may one day lead us to victory.

For, remember this, France does not stand alone. She is not isolated. Behind her is a vast empire, and she can make common cause with the British empire, which commands the seas and is continuing the struggle. Like England, she can draw unreservedly on the immense industrial resources of the United States.

This war is not limited to our unfortunate country.

The outcome of the struggle has not been decided by the battle of France. This is a world war. Mistakes have been made, there have been delays and untold suffering, but the fact remains that there still exists in the world everything we need to crush our enemies some day.

Today, we are crushed by the sheer weight of mechanized force hurled against us, but we can still look to a future in which even greater mechanized force will bring us victory. The destiny of the world is at stake.

I, General de Gaulle, now in London, call on all French officers and men who are at present on British soil, or may be in the future, with or without their arms; I call on all engineers and skilled workmen from the armaments factories who are at present on British soil, or may be in the future, to get in touch with me.

Whatever happens, the flame of French resistance must not and shall not die.

—— THE CONSEQUENCES ——

De Gaulle's appeal was not widely heard, but his message of refusal to submit to the Germans made him the figurehead of Free France. His radio broadcasts showed that the cause was not lost, despite the dire nature of France's situation. Back home, Germany had occupied northern France, and Pétain led a collaborationist regime in the south from the town of Vichy. Inspired by de Gaulle, thousands of French men and women joined the resistance, while many more joined the Free French Forces abroad. For his rebellious activities, the Vichy regime sentenced de Gaulle to death, in absentia, for treason. With British support, de Gaulle and his family set up home in the UK.

After the D–Day landings in Normandy, de Gaulle led the Free French Army in their liberation of Paris. When the war ended, elections were held in October 1945, and de Gaulle was made head of government. He resigned the next January, frustrated at the limits to his executive power. De Gaulle returned to power as president in 1958, and served until 1969. Under his leadership, he laid the foundations for the European Union by signing treaties with West Germany. In 1970, de Gaulle died suddenly at his country estate. The nation mourned their champion and liberator.

D-Day Order

Dwight D. Eisenhower (1890–1969) oversaw one of the most complicated and demanding military manoeuvres in history: the landing of over one million men in Normandy. On 6 June 1944, known as D-Day, Eisenhower issued an order to his invading army to 'bring about the destruction of the German war machine, the elimination of Nazi tyranny over the oppressed peoples of Europe, and security for ourselves in a free world'. He ended: 'The free men of the world are marching together to victory. I have full confidence in your courage, devotion to duty, and skill in battle. We will accept nothing less than full victory.' The D-Day landings, though they caused high numbers of casualties, were ultimately successful. Eisenhower then led the Allies in their liberation of the rest of France. His success as a leader saw him go on to win the presidency twice, and he is remembered as one of America's finest generals and most trusted figureheads.

1941
A DATE WHICH WILL
LIVE IN INFAMY

FRANKLIN D. ROOSEVELT
(1882–1945)

The Japanese attack on Pearl Harbor sent the United States hurtling headlong into the maelstrom of global war, and their vast resources, economic and military, would ultimately prove pivotal to the Allied victory. Franklin D. Roosevelt had been president since 1933, and helped to pull his country out of the Great Depression. Even though many at home were isolationists, believing the nation should stay out of the war, Roosevelt had sent aide to the Allies and begun building up the American military.

The raid on Pearl Harbor came as a shock to the Americans, even though relations with the Japanese had been tense for years owing to the US support of China in their conflict with Japan. In 1941, Roosevelt attempted to thwart Japanese ambitions further by cutting off vital oil supplies that they needed to continue their war. The conquest of the natural resource-rich Dutch East Indies (modern-day Indonesia) and British-controlled Malaya would solve the problem for Japan, but the American fleet, stationed in Hawaii, posed a potential threat to this plan. A preemptive strike would take them out of the war.

On the morning of 7 December 1941, the first wave of Japanese airplanes attacked Pearl Harbor. Sixteen American ships were destroyed or damaged and hundreds were killed. The next day, Roosevelt addressed Congress, to ask for their approval to declare war on the Japanese Empire.

—— THE SPEECH ——

Yesterday, December 7, 1941 – a date which will live in infamy – the United States of America was suddenly and deliberately attacked by naval and air forces of the Empire of Japan.

[. . .]

It will be recorded that the distance of Hawaii from Japan makes it obvious that the attack was deliberately planned many days or even weeks ago. During the intervening time, the Japanese Government has deliberately sought to deceive the United States by false statements and expressions of hope for continued peace.

The attack yesterday on the Hawaiian Islands has caused severe damage to American naval and military forces. I regret to tell you that very many American lives have been lost. In addition, American ships have been reported torpedoed on the high seas between San Francisco and Honolulu.

Yesterday, the Japanese Government also launched an attack against Malaya.

Last night, Japanese forces attacked Hong Kong.

Last night, Japanese forces attacked Guam.

Last night, Japanese forces attacked the Philippine Islands.

Last night, the Japanese attacked Wake Island. And this morning, the Japanese attacked Midway Island.

Japan has, therefore, undertaken a surprise offensive extending throughout the Pacific area. The facts of yesterday and today speak for themselves. The people of the United States have already formed their opinions and well understand the implications to the very life and safety of our Nation.

As Commander-in-Chief of the Army and Navy, I have directed that all measures be taken for our defense.

But always will our whole Nation remember the character of the onslaught against us.

No matter how long it may take us to overcome this

premeditated invasion, the American people in their righteous might will win through to absolute victory. I believe that I interpret the will of the Congress and of the people when I assert that we will not only defend ourselves to the uttermost but will make it very certain that this form of treachery shall never again endanger us.

Hostilities exist. There is no blinking at the fact that our people, our territory, and our interests are in grave danger.

With confidence in our armed forces – with the unbounding determination of our people – we will gain the inevitable triumph, so help us God.

I ask that the Congress declare that since the unprovoked and dastardly attack by Japan on Sunday, December 7, 1941, a state of war has existed between the United States and the Japanese Empire.

—— THE CONSEQUENCES ——

Within hours, Congress approved the declaration of war on Japan. On 11 December, Japan's allies, Germany and Italy, also declared war on the United States, and Roosevelt was faced with the prospect of global war. He handled it with the dedication and vigour he had shown throughout his political career, forging important connections with his fellow Allied leaders Stalin and, particularly, Churchill.

The first months of the war went badly for the United States. The attack on Pearl Harbor had meant Japan was able to establish itself as the dominant power in Southeast Asia. But the United States recovered from the onslaught and, in June 1942, won a stunning victory over the Japanese navy at the Battle of Midway, and began to claw back naval dominance of the Pacific. The Allies began the bloody process of winning back the islands and territories Japan had conquered. Meanwhile, American soldiers helped to liberate Western Europe from the Axis, as the Soviets did the same in the East.

In November 1944, Roosevelt won an unprecedented fourth term in office. He would not see his term out. Roosevelt had been paralyzed from the waist down since an attack from an unknown illness in 1921. The use of leg braces and a cane had allowed him to hide his disability from the public, but as the war entered its closing months, Roosevelt appeared increasingly ill and frail. Running the war had taken its toll. Roosevelt died of a massive stroke on 12 April 1945, a month before Germany capitulated. In the aftermath of the nuclear strikes on Hiroshima and Nagasaki, Japan surrendered on 9 August.

Surrender Ceremony on USS *Missouri*

After the attack on Pearl Harbor, the Japanese Empire began landing troops on the Philippines, which was an American dependency. The commander of US forces in the region was Douglas MacArthur (1880–1964), who had won merit for his service during World War I. MacArthur was unable to hold back the Japanese advance, and retreated to Australia in March 1942, vowing to return. He led the fight against the Japanese in the Pacific and landed in the Philippines again in October 1944, overseeing the liberation of the islands.

On 2 September 1945, MacArthur formally accepted the Japanese surrender aboard the USS *Missouri,* stating that 'both victors and vanquished . . . rise to that higher dignity which alone befits the sacred purposes we are about to serve: committing all our people unreservedly to faithful compliance with the understanding they are here formally to assume.' He hoped that 'from this solemn occasion a better world shall emerge out of the blood and carnage of the past – a world dedicated to the dignity of man and the fulfillment of his most cherished wish for freedom, tolerance and justice'. MacArthur commanded the Allied occupation of Japan and helped to oversee its reconstruction.

1941

ADDRESS ON THE ANNIVERSARY OF THE OCTOBER REVOLUTION

JOSEPH STALIN

(1878–1953)

When Lenin died in 1924, Joseph Vissarionovich Dzhugashvili – known as Stalin (the Russian word for 'steel') – became one of the most important leaders of the Soviet Union. He wanted absolute power, and orchestrated a Great Purge of any potential rivals in the late 1930s. Tens of thousands of people were killed, often under the flimsiest of pretenses. Crucially, many officers in the Red Army were eliminated, depriving it of experienced leadership. This was the least of Stalin's concerns: on 23 August, 1939 Nazi Germany and the Soviet Union signed a non-aggression treaty, the Molotov-Ribbentrop Pact. Its terms also secretly carved up Eastern Europe between the Nazis and the Soviets. On 17 September, the

Soviets invaded eastern Poland. Stalin brutally crushed any potential resistance, and approved the killing of over 25,000 Polish prisoners-of-war at the Katyn Massacre. With war raging across Western Europe, he appeared to have secured peace for his country.

This illusory safety was shattered on 22 June 1941, when Adolf Hitler launched Operation Barbarossa, a massed coordinated invasion of Soviet territory. The 'Great Patriotic War' had begun. To slow the Germans down, Stalin ordered a 'scorched earth' policy to destroy anything of possible use to the invaders. However, nothing seemed able to stop the fascist juggernaut. By autumn, they had conquered Kiev, besieged Leningrad (Saint Petersburg), and begun the push towards Moscow. On 7 November, Stalin addressed the crowds at the Red Square in Moscow, on the anniversary of the revolution that had effectively established communist rule.

—— THE SPEECH ——

. . . Comrades, today we must celebrate the twenty-fourth anniversary of the October Revolution in difficult conditions. The German brigands' treacherous attack and the war that they forced upon us have created a threat to our country. We have temporarily lost a number of regions, and the enemy is before the gates of Leningrad and Moscow.

The enemy calculated that our army would be dispersed at the very first blow and our country forced to its knees. But the enemy wholly miscalculated. Despite temporary reverses, our army and our navy are bravely beating off enemy attacks along the whole front, inflicting heavy losses, while our country – our whole country – has organized itself into a single fighting camp in order, jointly with our army and navy, to rout the German invaders.

[. . .]

Our whole country, all the peoples of our country, are backing our army and our navy, helping them smash the Nazi hordes. Our reserves in manpower are inexhaustible. The spirit of the great Lenin inspires us for our patriotic war today as it did twenty-three years ago.

[. . .]

Comrades, Red Army and Red Navy men, commanders and political instructors, men and women guerrillas! The whole world is looking to you as a force capable of destroying the brigand hordes of German invaders. The enslaved peoples of Europe under the yoke of the German invaders are looking to you as their liberators. A great mission of liberation has fallen to your lot. Be worthy of this mission! The war you are waging is a war of liberation, a just war. Let the heroic images of our great ancestors [. . .] inspire you in this war! Let the victorious banner of the great Lenin fly over your heads! Utter destruction to the German invaders! Death to the German armies of occupation! Long live our glorious motherland, her freedom and her independence! Under the banner of Lenin – onward to victory!

—— THE CONSEQUENCES ——

Stalin reminded his listeners that the Soviet Union had been on the edge of destruction in its early years, during the Russian Civil War, and had survived – it would do so again. In December 1941, with the Germans within twenty miles of Moscow, the Soviets won their first major victory – pushing them back from the capital. The German army began to suffer in the cold Russian winter and faced major supply problems. The Soviets, though initially outnumbered, started to bring their huge population advantage to bear. Stalin had also relocated important factories east, out of range of the Germans, ensuring the Red Army continual supplies, while within the army he enforced strict discipline.

Eventually, Stalin shifted his aim from survival to victory. The Soviets triumphed at the bloody Battle of

Stalingrad, and followed with a major victory at Kursk, the largest tank battle in history. The resurgent Red Army forced the Nazis out of Russian territory and back into Germany. On 2 May 1945, Berlin surrendered to the Soviets and, six days later, the war in Europe was over.

Victory had cost the Soviet Union the lives of millions of soldiers and citizens. Then on, Stalin set about ensuring Soviet dominance in post-war Eastern Europe – much to the chagrin of Britain and the United States. An 'iron curtain', as Churchill termed it, had fallen across Europe.

1943
DO YOU WANT
TOTAL WAR?

JOSEPH GOEBBELS
(1897–1945)

Joseph Goebbels worked as a journalist and writer before joining the Nazis in 1924. Adept at winning public support through rallies, radio broadcasts and film, and with an unquestioning loyalty to Hitler, Goebbels became part of the inner circle and quickly rose up the party ranks.

After the Nazis came to national power, Goebbels was made Minister for Public Enlightenment and Propaganda. He used the position to gain unprecedented control of all aspects of German culture and, in 1938, he orchestrated *Kristallnacht*, a violent assault on Jewish people, businesses and synagogues.

After the war began in 1939, Goebbels became increasingly influential in national politics. By 1943, the Nazi war effort had comprehensively stalled. Severe shortages of fuel and food, Allied bombing raids, and the crushing defeat at Stalingrad meant public confidence was waning. On 18 February, Goebbels addressed a large audience at the Sportpalast meeting hall in Berlin. He sought to quash any talk of a decline in public morale and remind the German people that only victory could save Germany from disaster and Europe from 'Bolshevist-Jewish slavery'. Most of all, Goebbels demanded total commitment to the war effort.

—— THE SPEECH ——

. . . Do you want total war? If necessary, do you want a war more total and radical than anything we can even imagine today?

[. . .]

With burning hearts and cool heads we will overcome the major problems of this phase of the war. We are on the way to final victory. That victory rests on our faith in the Führer.

This evening, I once again remind the whole nation of its duty. The Führer expects us to do that which will throw all we have done in the past into the shadows.

We do not want to fail him. As we are proud of him, he should be proud of us.

The great crises and upsets of national life show who the true men and women are. We have no right any longer to speak of the weaker sex, for both sexes are displaying the same determination and spiritual strength. The nation is ready for anything. The Führer has commanded, and we will follow him. In this hour of national reflection and contemplation, we believe firmly and unshakably in victory. We see it before us, we need only reach for it. We must resolve to subordinate everything to it. That is the duty of the hour. Let the slogan be:

'Now, people rise up and let the storm break loose!'

—— THE CONSEQUENCES ——

Goebbels's plan to involve every German citizen in the war effort was not fully embraced by Hitler and other Nazi leaders, who did not want all women to be recruited in the workforce. Still, Goebbels continued to strive to bolster German morale in the face of an unravelling war effort. With Hitler's public appearances becoming increasingly rare, Goebbels became one of the most high-profile Nazi leaders. In 1944, Hitler made Goebbels the 'Reich Plenipotentiary for Total War'.

One year after his speech, Goebbels was able to try to

put the philosophy into motion. All able-bodied men were to either serve in the armed forces or work in armaments factories. One of the chief consequences of the Total War philosophy was the recruitment of ever-younger members of the Hitler Youth into the armed forces. Desperate shortages of manpower meant that even boys of twelve were forced to fight.

But it was too late to save the Nazis from defeat. As the Allies closed in on Berlin, Hitler announced he would remain in the capital until death. Unlike other Nazi leaders, Goebbels resolved to remain by Hitler's side until the bitter end. He moved his wife and their six children into Hitler's bunker complex. When Hitler made his final will and testament, Goebbels was one of the witnesses.

After Hitler committed suicide on 30 April, under the terms of the will, Goebbels inherited the title of Reich Chancellor. It was an empty office. By now, the Soviets had entered Berlin and there was fighting on the streets. Goebbels would not leave and, on 1 May, he and his wife drugged their children and then killed them with cyanide capsules. They then committed suicide, rather than fall into the hands of the Soviets.

1944
SERVE THE PEOPLE

MAO ZEDONG
(1893–1976)

Mao Zedong was China's first communist ruler and oversaw its transformation from a war-torn, divided republic into a single-party authoritarian state. Mao had been involved in the Chinese Communist Party since its foundation. The Communists had struggled, often violently, with the Nationalist Kuomintang for control of China. In 1934, the Communist armies embarked from the south on the 'Long March' to escape the Kuomintang armies. It was Mao's leadership that guaranteed their survival, and established him as the most important Communist leader.

However, Mao still faced the threat of war with Japan, who had conquered Manchuria in Northeast China in 1931/2 and had ambitions for further expansion into China. Mao came to believe that the only way to defeat the Japanese was for the Communists to ally with the Kuomintang and its leader Chiang Kai-shek, which they did in 1936.

The next year, open war broke out between Japan and China. The Chinese suffered a series of losses but the Japanese were unable to decisively defeat them. The two main Communist fighting forces were the Eighth Route and New Fourth Armies. While fighting the Japanese, the Communists also faced sporadic violence from the Kuomintang. On 8 September 1944, Mao delivered a speech in memory of Zhang Side, a loyal comrade who had taken part in the Long March and served as one of Mao's bodyguards. He died when an opium-producing kiln collapsed on him.

—— THE SPEECH ——

Our Communist Party and the Eighth Route and New Fourth Armies led by our Party are battalions of the revolution. These battalions of ours are wholly dedicated to the liberation of the people and work entirely in the people's interests. Comrade Zhang Side was in the ranks of these battalions.

[. . .]

To die for the people is weightier than Mount Tai, but to work for the fascists and die for the exploiters and oppressors is lighter than a feather. Comrade Zhang Side died for the people, and his death is indeed weightier than Mount Tai.

[. . .]

We hail from all corners of the country and have joined together for a common revolutionary objective. And we need the vast majority of the people with us on the road to this objective. Today, we already lead base areas with a population of ninety-one million, but this is not enough; to liberate the whole nation more are needed. In times of difficulty, we must not lose sight of our achievements, must see the bright future and must pluck up our courage. The Chinese people are suffering; it is our duty to save them and we must exert ourselves in struggle. Wherever there is struggle there is sacrifice, and death is a common occurrence. But we have the interests of the people and the sufferings of the great majority at heart, and when we die for the people it is a worthy death. Nevertheless, we should do our best to avoid unnecessary sacrifices. Our cadres must show concern for every soldier, and all people in the revolutionary ranks must care for each other, must love and help each other.

The exhortation to 'serve the people' became a key Maoist slogan. With the support of the public, the Communists gained control of the countryside and defeated the Kuomintang. In 1945, the Japanese surrendered. But peace did not last: civil war broke out between the Communists and the Kuomintang the following year. Mao's Red Army emerged victorious from the struggle, and the People's Republic of China was founded on 1 October 1949. Chiang Kai-shek and the rest of the Kuomintang leadership and supporters fled to the island of Taiwan, where they established a separate Republic of China.

Mao set about reforming the nation. Starting in 1953, Mao's two Five-Year Plans were designed to turn China into a modern industrial power. In the process, however, millions of people died, many of them from famine, as Chinese society and economy was profoundly and recklessly destabilized. In 1966, Mao launched the Cultural Revolution, which was an attempt to purge China of any elements of pre-Communist society. This led to the deaths of hundreds of thousands of people.

Mao died in 1976. Despite the fact that he owed his success to the support of the Chinese people, his personal rule had been responsible for the deaths of millions.

MAO ZEDONG

Celebrating the Founding of the
People's Republic of China

Zhou Enlai (1898–1976) was one of Mao's most trusted political allies and effective negotiators. When Mao initiated the Cultural Revolution in 1966, Zhou at first opposed it. He disagreed with Mao's plans to completely purge China of any remnants of the old society and ensure that the leadership was ideologically pure. But to ensure his political survival, he reversed his criticism, publicly supporting Mao in a speech on the seventeenth anniversary of the founding of the People's Republic of China, given on 30 September 1966. He announced that the 'Cultural Revolution has [. . .] defeated the arrogance of the reactionary bourgeoisie and is cleaning up all the rubbish left over by the old society'. Zhou argued that Mao's leadership was essential to China: 'we shall certainly succeed in building up our great motherland and in making it an impregnable proletarian state that will never change colour'. The Cultural Revolution devastated the lives of many: hundreds of thousands were executed and millions were forced to move to rural areas. Zhou continued to serve as Mao's top diplomat; however, their relationship slowly deteriorated and, when Zhou died in 1976, Mao made no public tribute to the man who had served him for decades.

1945

DECLARATION OF
INDEPENDENCE

HO CHI MINH
(1890–1969)

When Ho Chi Minh was born, Vietnam was part of French Indochina, which also covered Cambodia and Laos. The French refused to allow the Vietnamese people self-government. Ho, who had trained as a cook, left Vietnam in his early twenties as a galley hand on a ship. He lived and worked in several countries, including the United States, England, France, the Soviet Union and China. While abroad, Ho became involved in organized communist politics.

In 1940, the Japanese invaded Vietnam and occupied it. Ho returned to his homeland in 1941 and, together with other communists, formed the Vietminh – a group fighting for the freedom of the country. The Vietminh launched a guerrilla campaign (with support from the American Office of Strategic Services, the precursor to the CIA) against the Japanese occupiers. In August 1945, the Japanese in Vietnam were defeated. On 2 September, Ho made a declaration of Vietnamese independence at Ba Dinh Square in Hanoi.

— THE SPEECH —

'All men are created equal. They are endowed by their Creator with certain unalienable Rights; among these are Life, Liberty, and the pursuit of Happiness.' This immortal statement was made in the Declaration of Independence of the United States of America in 1776. In a broader sense, this means: all the peoples on the earth are equal from birth, all the peoples have a right to live, to be happy and free. The Declaration of the French Revolution made in 1791 on the Rights of Man and the citizen also states: 'All men are born free and with equal rights, and must always remain free and have equal rights.' These are undeniable truths. Nevertheless, for more than eighty years, the French imperialists, abusing the standard of Liberty, Equality and Fraternity, have violated our Fatherland and oppressed our fellow citizens. They have acted contrary to the ideals of humanity and justice. In the field of politics, they have deprived our people of every democratic liberty.

[. . .]

They have built more prisons than schools. They have mercilessly slain our patriots; they have drowned our uprisings in rivers of blood [. . .] In the field of economics, they have fleeced us to the backbone, impoverished our people and devastated our land [. . .] The whole Vietnamese people, animated by a common purpose, are determined to fight to the bitter end against any attempt by the French colonialists to reconquer their country.

[. . .]

A people who have courageously opposed French domination for more than eighty years, a people who have fought side by side with the Allies against the fascists during these last years, such a people must be free and independent. For these reasons, we, members of the Provisional Government of the Democratic Republic of Vietnam, solemnly declare to the world that Vietnam has the right to be a free and independent country – and in fact, it is so already. The entire Vietnamese people are determined to mobilize all their physical and mental strength, to sacrifice their lives and property in order to safeguard their independence and liberty.

Ho's declaration was not recognized. After World War II ended, France was determined to restore its colonial rule of Vietnam, and sent in armed forces to regain control. After four years of conflict with the Japanese, Ho had another war to fight. The Vietminh, with Soviet backing, grew from a guerrilla force to an organized, modern army. At the 1954 Battle of Dien Bien Phu, the Vietminh decisively defeated the French, who were forced to leave Vietnam.

As part of the peace talks ending the war, Vietnam was divided in two. Ho led North Vietnam, establishing a communist state and violently suppressing any opposition groups. South Vietnam became a repressive military dictatorship supported by the United States. Opposing this regime in the South, with Ho's support and guidance, were the Vietcong. Fearing a communist takeover of South Vietnam, the American government sent ground troops into Vietnam in 1965. Despite their seemingly overwhelming military might, the Americans were unable to defeat the communist forces. As the 1960s drew to an end, it became increasingly clear that Ho would be victorious.

Ho did not live to see ultimate victory and the unification of Vietnam. He died of a heart attack in 1969 and his body was displayed in the very square in Hanoi where he had declared Vietnam's independence.

The Great Silent Majority

Richard Nixon (1913–94), who had served as Eisenhower's vice-president, won the presidential election in 1968, during the Vietnam War. When he took up office in 1969, there were over half a million American troops in Vietnam. Thirty-one thousand had been killed in the war. Nixon started peace talks with North Vietnam in Paris. He pursued a policy of 'Viet-namization' of the war – gradually withdrawing American troops and replacing them with South Vietnamese forces. Heavy bombing campaigns continued.

On 3 September 1969, Nixon addressed the American public, asking for their support. He appealed to the 'great silent majority' of Americans, saying, 'the more divided we are at home, the less likely the enemy is to negotiate in Paris'. Nixon urged the American people to be 'united for peace [. . .] united against defeat'.

As negotiations in Paris dragged on, the war continued. Nixon was re-elected president in 1972. The next year, the Paris Peace Accords were signed, signalling the withdrawal of American troops. The South Vietnamese were overwhelmed and defeated in 1975. The communists had won the war, and united north and south in 1976. Nixon, mired in the Watergate scandal, was forced to resign from the presidency in 1974.

1948
IF WE HAVE ARMS
TO FIGHT WITH

GOLDA MEIR

(1898–1978)

Golda Meir was born in Kiev, but her family
emigrated to the United States to escape anti-
Semitic violence. There, Meir became involved in
Zionism, the movement to establish a Jewish homeland
in Palestine. In 1921, she moved to Palestine, which, at
the time, was administered by Britain, to join a kibbutz.
The British struggled to keep peace between the
Palestinian Arabs and Jewish settlers; violence and
rioting between the three factions were commonplace.
Meir became one of the most influential Jewish leaders
in Palestine.

In 1947, Britain agreed to cede control of Palestine
to the United Nations. Their plan for Palestine was to

partition it into separate Arab and Jewish states. Neither faction fully backed the plan. When the United Nations formally voted to adopt it on 30 November, the simmering violence in Palestine escalated into civil war. The British, who were in the process of arranging their withdrawal, made no concerted effort to put an end to the violence.

In 1948, Meir travelled to the United States, to gather donations to buy more weapons and armaments to protect the 700,000 Jewish settlers in Palestine. On 2 January, she addressed the Council of Jewish Federations in Chicago.

—— THE SPEECH ——

I have had the privilege of representing Palestine Jewry in this country and in other countries when the problems that we faced were those of building more kibbutzim, of bringing in more Jews in spite of political obstacles and Arab riots. We always had faith that in the end we would win, that everything we were doing in the country led to the independence of the Jewish people and to a Jewish state. Long before we had dared pronounce that word, we knew what was in store for us. Today, we have reached a point when the nations of the world have given us their decision – the establishment of a Jewish state in a part of Palestine.

Now in Palestine we are fighting to make this resolution of the United Nations a reality, not because we wanted to fight. If we had the choice, we would have chosen peace to build in peace. We have no alternative.

[. . .]

I want to say to you, friends, that the Jewish community in Palestine is going to fight to the very end. If we have arms to fight with, we will fight with those, and if not, we will fight with stones in our hands.

[. . .]

My friends, we are at war. There is no Jew in Palestine who does not believe that finally we will be victorious. That is the spirit of the country . . . We know what happened to the Jews of Europe during this last war. And every Jew in the country also knows that within a few months a Jewish state in Palestine will be established. We knew that the price we would have to pay would be the best of our people. There are over 300 killed by now. There will be more. There is no doubt that there will be more. But there is also no doubt that the spirit of our young people is such that no matter how many Arabs invade the country, their spirit will not falter. However, this valiant spirit alone cannot face rifles and machine-guns. Rifles and machine-guns without spirit are not worth very much, but spirit without arms can in time be broken with the body.

[. . .]

I have spoken to you without a grain of exaggeration. I have not tried to paint the picture in false colours. It consists of spirit and certainty of our victory on the one hand, and dire necessity for carrying on the battle on the other.

—— THE CONSEQUENCES ——

Meir's trip was a huge success: she raised fifty million dollars. The money would prove to be crucial. On 14 May, Israel declared independence and Meir was one of the signatories of the declaration. The next day, a coalition of Arab nations converged on the new nation. The Israelis were able to hold out against the attack. A twenty-eight-day truce was declared in June, but both sides used the break in fighting to buy more arms and bring in more men. When fighting restarted, the Israelis took the initiative. After another truce between July and October, the fighting continued until March 1949. The Israeli state had survived but at the cost of thousands of lives. The money raised by Meir's efforts in the United States had been essential. David Ben-Gurion, Israel's first Prime Minister, stated that 'someday, when history will be written, it will be said that there was a Jewish woman who got the money which made the state possible'.

After the war, Meir continued her involvement in government, becoming Israel's new leader in 1969. She was to face many more challenges in her career, but continued to safeguard her nation. She died in 1978, her importance in the foundation of Israel undoubted.

1954
I AM AWARE THAT THIS
IS A HARD DOCTRINE

SYNGMAN RHEE
(1875–1965)

After World War II, Korea was liberated from Japanese rule. The United Nations divided the Korean Peninsula into North Korea, a single-party communist state backed by the Soviet Union, and South Korea, a democratic nation. South Korea's first leader, installed by the Americans, was Syngman Rhee. He had lived in the United States for many years after fleeing Korea as a young man, and was well known in the West as a campaigner for Korean independence and unification. He was also a virulent anti-communist.

In 1948, Rhee was elected president of South Korea. His rule was virtually dictatorial. Communists and other opposition groups were the subject of violent oppression, and thousands were killed.

In 1950, the North Koreans invaded the South, and conquered Seoul after three days of war. Rhee fled the capital. The United Nations sent a multinational force to Korea, while China sent troops to support North Korea.

After months of fighting, the war reached a stalemate and an armistice was declared in 1953. The pre-war border was restored and flanked by a four-kilometre (2.5-mile)-wide demilitarized zone. In 1954, Rhee made a trip to the United States to lobby for the unification of all Korea and the destruction of worldwide communism. On 28 July, Rhee addressed Congress. He refused any offers from advisers to check his speech, saying, 'I came to America to speak my own mind . . . and I'm going to do it – in my own way.'

—— THE SPEECH ——

On the Korean front, the guns are silent for the moment, stilled temporarily by the unwise armistice which the enemy is using to build up his strength. Now that the Geneva Conference has come to an end with no result, as predicted, it is quite in place to declare the end of the armistice.

[. . .]

Within a few years, the Soviet Union will possess the means to vanquish the United States. We must act now. Where can we act? We can act in the Far East [...] the Korean front comprises only one small portion of the war we want to win – the war for Asia, the war for the world, the war for freedom on earth.

[...]

The return of the Chinese mainland to the side of the free world would automatically produce a victorious end to the wars in Korea and Indochina and would swing the balance of power so that the Soviets would not dare to rise war with the United States. Unless we win China back, an ultimate victory for the free world is unthinkable. Soviet troops might intervene to defend China, but that would be excellent for the free world, since it would justify the destruction of Soviet centres of production by the American Air Force before the Soviet hydrogen bombs had been produced in quantity. I am aware that this is a hard doctrine. But the Communists have made this a hard world, a horrible world, in which to be soft is to become a slave [...] let us remember [...] that peace cannot be restored in this world half Communist and half democratic. Your momentous decision is needed now to make Asia safe for freedom, for that will automatically settle the world Communist problem in Europe, Africa and America.

Rhee's uncompromising message, particularly the suggestion to attack China, shocked his listeners. The reaction to the speech was generally negative, and Rhee later called it the 'worst mistake' of his life. The United States did not restart hostilities against North Korea, and the peninsula continued to be divided.

Rhee returned home as president and continued his oppressive rule, even changing the constitution to allow him to run for president an unlimited number of times.

In 1960, Rhee won a fourth term as president amid rumours that he had fixed the vote. A wave of rebellion swept the nation. The police clashed with protestors and fired on them. Student groups led a campaign to overthrow Rhee, and he eventually resigned on 26 April. He left Korea for exile in Hawaii, where he died after a stroke in 1965. South Korea faced years of instability and military rule, making the transition to democracy in 1987.

1971
THE STRUGGLE THIS
TIME IS THE STRUGGLE
FOR INDEPENDENCE

SHEIKH MUJIBUR RAHMAN
(1920–75)

The Partition of India created Pakistan – a separate homeland for Muslims. It stretched over modern-day Pakistan and Bangladesh. This system was unwieldy, as the new nation was divided into two halves separated by hundreds of miles. West Pakistan was dominant, despite being home to the minority of the population. The Bengali people of East Pakistan were marginalized politically and culturally.

Sheikh Mujibur Rahman was a member of the Awami League, a political organization that fought for more rights for East Pakistan. He had been arrested several times for his outspoken demands for autonomy, but was popular among the people for his refusal to back down.

WE SHALL FIGHT ON THE BEACHES

In 1970, elections were held in Pakistan. The Awami League won a majority, but the military regime ruling Pakistan, led by General Yahya Khan, refused to uphold the results. On 7 March 1971, Mujibur addressed a mass rally in Dhaka, at the Ramna Racecourse.

—— THE SPEECH ——

Struggle this time is the struggle for independence. Today, I come to you with a heavy heart. You know everything and understand as well. We tried our best. But the streets of Dhaka, Chittagong, Khulna, Rajshiahi and Rangpur have been dyed red with the blood of our brethren. People of Bangladesh today want liberation. They want to survive. They want to have their rights. What wrong did we do? In the elections, people of Bangladesh voted for me and the Awami League. We had a hope that we would sit in the assembly and frame a constitution which would lead to the emancipation of the people economically, politically and culturally.

[. . .]

Arms were used against the unarmed people of Bangladesh. The arms which were bought by our money, to safeguard the country from foreign aggression, are now being used to kill our poor people. My distressed people are being shot at. We are the majority in Pakistan. Whenever we, the Bengalis, wanted to take over power, wanted to become masters of our own destiny, they pounced on us – every time.

[. . .]

I request you to form action committees in every village, ward and union under the leadership of the Awami League. Prepare yourself with whatever you have. Remember, once we have shed our blood, we will not hesitate to shed more. But we will free the people of this country, Insha'Allah! The struggle this time is the struggle for freedom; the struggle this time is the struggle for independence.

—— THE CONSEQUENCES ——

Mujibur's exhortation for a mass uprising led to swift, violent repercussions. He declared East Pakistan to be independent and the new state was called Bangladesh. To regain control of the country, Khan unleashed Operation Searchlight. Martial law was declared and the Awami League was outlawed. Mujibur was arrested and transported to West Pakistan.

In their effort to subjugate the Bangladeshi bid for

independence, the Pakistani Army killed half a million people. Millions more Bangladeshis fled across the border to India. Supported by the Indian government, a resistance army called the Mukti Bahini battled against the Pakistani army in Bangladesh. As a result, war also broke out between Pakistan and India, and there was fighting on the border of these countries as well. On 16 December 1971, the overwhelmed Pakistani forces in Bangladesh surrendered. Nearly 100,000 of their troops were captured. They were returned home in 1972 as part of the peace treaty between India and Pakistan, which saw the latter power recognize Bangladesh as an independent nation.

Mujibur was released from captivity and returned to Bangladesh to become the nation's first president. He wanted to transform Bangladesh into a secular state and oversaw sweeping land reforms as well as the nationalization of many industries. Not everyone supported his regime. In 1975, he declared a state of emergency and began to crack down on opponents. All political parties but Mujibur's were declared illegal. Disgruntled army officers and former supporters planned a coup to overthrow Mujibur and, on 15 August, armed men raided his residence and assassinated him. Without strong leadership, the country descended into turmoil and faced years of coups and military rule, only returning to democracy in the 1990s.

A Tryst with Destiny

Jawaharlal Nehru (1889–1964) was the first prime minister of India and, along with Gandhi, was one of the most influential figures in the nonviolent struggle for Indian independence. After years of campaigning, the British passed the Indian Independence Act in 1947. One of the provisions was to create a separate homeland, Pakistan, in areas with a Muslim-majority population.

On the eve of Indian independence, Nehru addressed the nation's constituent assembly: 'Long years ago, we made a tryst with destiny, and now the time comes when we shall redeem our pledge [. . .] India will awake to life and freedom.' Nehru pledged to 'build up a prosperous, democratic and progressive nation'. He urged tolerance: 'All of us, to whatever religion we may belong, are equally the children of India with equal rights, privileges and obligations.'

This latter appeal was in vain. Over ten million Hindus and Muslims scrambled to flee from their homes to safety in India and Pakistan, respectively. The situation quickly descended into violence and thousands were attacked and killed. India and Pakistan went to war that October over control of the disputed province of Kashmir. The two nations would go on to fight three more wars.

1973

FAREWELL TO THE NATION

SALVADOR ALLENDE

(1908–73)

In 1970, Salvador Allende narrowly won the Chilean presidential election at his fourth attempt. A committed socialist who had close ties with the Communist Party, once in office, he nationalized many industries, including banking and copper mining, Chile's biggest export. He also established diplomatic relations with Communist Cuba and invited Fidel Castro to Chile for a state visit.

But Allende's radical agenda and left-wing beliefs posed a threat to American business and political interests in Chile. With President Nixon's approval, the CIA worked to destabilize Allende's regime by supporting and funding his opponents. Under Allende's rule, Chile's economy began to contract and prices rose.

Allende's critics became more vocal. In June 1973, an unsuccessful coup attempt was followed by a general strike. The Supreme Court questioned Allende's ability to rule. On 11 September, the armed forces, led by General Augusto Pinochet, launched a revolt against Allende. Within hours, the military junta had control of all of the country except the capital, Santiago.

With armed men advancing on the presidential palace, Allende addressed the nation via the radio. He had refused to flee, and vowed to fight – armed with an AK-47 given to him by Castro. As he said his farewell in a national radio address, gunfire and explosions could be heard in the background as forces loyal to Allende strove to fight back against the junta's men.

— THE SPEECH —

Surely, this will be the last opportunity for me to address you. The Air Force has bombed the antennas of Radio Magallanes. My words do not have bitterness but disappointment. May they be a moral punishment for those who have betrayed their oath [. . .] the only thing left for me is to say to workers: I am not going to resign! Placed in a historic transition, I will pay for loyalty to the people with my life. And I say to them that I am certain that the seeds which we have planted in the good conscience of thousands and thousands of

Chileans will not be shriveled forever. They have force and will be able to dominate us, but social processes can be arrested by neither crime nor force. History is ours, and people make history.

[. . .]

Surely, Radio Magallanes will be silenced, and the calm metal instrument of my voice will no longer reach you. It does not matter. You will continue hearing it. I will always be next to you. At least my memory will be that of a man of dignity who was loyal to his country. The people must defend themselves, but they must not sacrifice themselves. The people must not let themselves be destroyed or riddled with bullets, but they cannot be humiliated either.

Workers of my country, I have faith in Chile and its destiny. Other men will overcome this dark and bitter moment when treason seeks to prevail. Keep in mind that, much sooner than later, great avenues will again be opened, through which will pass the free man, to construct a better society. Long live Chile! Long live the people! Long live the workers! These are my last words, and I am certain that my sacrifice will not be in vain, I am certain that, at the very least, it will be a moral lesson that will punish felony, cowardice and treason.

—— THE CONSEQUENCES ——

That afternoon Pinochet's troops, with air support, forced the surrender of the beleaguered presidential palace. Allende lay dead. The junta claimed he had committed suicide, whereas Allende's supporters claimed he was killed in the fighting. Subsequent forensic analysis has still not led to a conclusive answer. Regardless, the junta now controlled all of Chile.

Pinochet established a military dictatorship, suspending elected bodies and trade unions. Thousands of Chileans suspected of opposing the regime – the 'disappeared' – were imprisoned and killed.

In 1988, a national vote revealed that the majority of Chileans did not support Pinochet's presidency. The man who had come to power amid violence and bloodshed peacefully stepped down in 1990. Chile returned to democracy after nearly thirty years of dictatorship.

1987
TEAR DOWN
THIS WALL!

RONALD REAGAN
(1911–2004)

After World War II, the United States and the Soviet Union were the two most important and powerful nations in the world. Holding diametrically opposed philosophies, both states had the military capability to completely destroy each other – and the rest of the planet as well. Relations between the United States and the Soviet Union often became heated, but the 'Cold War' never broke out into open conflict between the two superpowers.

In 1980, Ronald Reagan won the American presidential election. Reagan was staunchly anti-Communist and outspoken about his views, claiming that the philosophy of Marxism-Leninism would be left on the 'ash heap of history' and referring to the Soviet Union as an 'evil empire'. He actively built up American military power to put pressure on the Soviets, and set up the 'Star Wars' initiative, which would use space-based technology to protect the United States from missile attack. In 1984, Reagan was re-elected in a landslide victory.

Meanwhile, the Soviet Union was disintegrating. Its economy was slowly collapsing and three of its leaders died in under three years. In 1985, Mikhail Gorbachev came to power. Gorbachev was a reformer, who would launch the policies of *perestroika* ('restructuring') and *glasnost* ('transparency'), which liberalized Soviet society, economy and media. Gorbachev also took part in successful talks with Reagan that led to the scaling back of both countries' nuclear capabilities.

In 1987, Reagan visited Berlin to take part in the celebrations of the seven hundred and fiftieth anniversary of the city's official founding. The Berlin Wall, constructed by East German authorities in 1961, divided the city – and was a visual reminder of Communist domination over Eastern Europe. In a speech at the Brandenburg Gate near the Wall, Reagan called on Gorbachev to hasten his reforms.

—— THE SPEECH——

. . . Our gathering today is being broadcast throughout Western Europe and North America. I understand that it is being seen and heard as well in the East. To those listening throughout Eastern Europe, I extend my warmest greetings and the goodwill of the American people. To those listening in East Berlin, a special word: Although I cannot be with you, I address my remarks to you just as surely as to those standing here before me. For I join you, as I join your fellow countrymen in the West, in this firm, this unalterable belief: *Es gibt nur ein Berlin*. ('There is only one Berlin.')

Behind me stands a wall that encircles the free sectors of this city, part of a vast system of barriers that divides the entire continent of Europe. From the Baltic South, those barriers cut across Germany in a gash of barbed wire, concrete, dog runs and guard towers. Farther south, there may be no visible, no obvious wall. But there remain armed guards and checkpoints all the same – still a restriction on the right to travel, still an instrument to impose upon ordinary men and women the will of a totalitarian state.

Yet, it is here in Berlin where the wall emerges most clearly; here, cutting across your city, where the news photo and the television screen have imprinted this brutal division of a continent upon the mind of the world.

Standing before the Brandenburg Gate, every man is a German separated from his fellow man.

Every man is a Berliner, forced to look upon a scar.

WE SHALL FIGHT ON THE BEACHES

[. . .]

General Secretary Gorbachev, if you seek peace, if you seek prosperity for the Soviet Union and Eastern Europe, if you seek liberalization: Come here to this gate.

Mr Gorbachev, open this gate.

Mr Gorbachev – Mr Gorbachev, tear down this wall!

[. . .]

In Europe, only one nation and those it controls refuse to join the community of freedom. Yet in this age of redoubled economic growth, of information and innovation, the Soviet Union faces a choice: It must make fundamental changes, or it will become obsolete.

Today, thus, represents a moment of hope. We in the West stand ready to cooperate with the East to promote true openness, to break down barriers that separate people, to create a safer, freer world. And surely, there is no better place than Berlin, the meeting place of East and West, to make a start.

—— THE CONSEQUENCES——

In the aftermath of Reagan's speech in Berlin, Gorbachev further liberalized the Soviet Union. In 1988, Reagan and Gorbachev met in Moscow for more talks on nuclear disarmament. The next year, Reagan's final term ended and he retired to California to be succeeded by his vice-president, George H. W. Bush.

In 1989, communist regimes in Soviet satellite states in Eastern Europe began to be overthrown under pressure from mass public protest. In November that year, the Berlin Wall was torn down, and people were able to move freely between the formerly divided eastern and western sectors of the city. Germany was reunified in 1990.

The Soviet Union began to unravel, as its economy declined and its constituent republics began to agitate for more freedom and autonomy. On Christmas Day 1991, Gorbachev resigned. The next day, the Soviet Union's fifteen republics were granted independence and the nation was formally dissolved. The Cold War was over.

Reagan's energetic leadership in the closing years of the conflict had put major pressure on the communist regime, and helped contribute to its eventual collapse. Reagan died at home in 2004, after a long struggle with Alzheimer's. His state funeral in Washington was attended by dozens of world leaders and he remains one of the most influential statesmen of the twentieth century.

SOURCES

Pericles: Jowett, Benjamin (trans.) Thucydides' *The History of the Peloponnesian War* (1881)

Alexander the Great: http://www.fordham.edu/halsall/ancient/arrian-alexander1.asp

Hannibal: Baker, George (trans.) Livy's *The History of Rome* (1823)

Julius Caesar: *Histories of Appian*, Loeb Classical Library (1913)

William the Conqueror: MacArthur, Brian (ed.) *The Penguin Book of Historic Speeches* (Penguin, 1996)

Pope Urban II: McNeal, Edgar Holmes and Thatcher, Oliver J. (eds) *A Source Book for Mediaeval History*, (Scribners, 1905)

Saladin:

http://www.fordham.edu/halsall/med/salahdin.asp

Emperor Constantine XI: Philippodes, M. (trans.), Sphrantzes, G. *The Fall of the Byzantine Empire: A Chronicle 1401–1477* (University of Massachusetts Press, 1980)

Hernán Cortés: Prescott, W. H. *The History of the Conquest of Mexico* (1843)

Elizabeth I: Rede, L. T. (ed.) *The Modern Speaker; Containing Selections from the Works of our Most Approved Authors* (1826)

Oliver Cromwell:

http://www.emersonkent.com/speeches/dismissal_of _the_rump_parliament.htm

James Francis Edward Stuart: Green, C. H. (ed.) Historical Register (1717)

Patrick Henry:

http://www.law.ou.edu/ushistory/henry.shtml

George Washington:

http://etc.usf.edu/lit2go/132/presidential-addresses-and-messages/5154/george-washington-prevents-the-revolt-of-his-officers-march-15-1783/

Maximilien de Robespierre:

http://chnm.gmu.edu/revolution/d/413/

Napoleon Bonaparte: Tarbell, I. M. (ed.) *Napoleon's Addresses: Selections from the Proclamations, Speeches and Correspondence of Napoleon Bonaparte* (Colonial Press, 1896)

SOURCES

Simón Bolívar:
http://www.fordham.edu/halsall/mod/1819bolivar.asp
Giuseppe Garibaldi:
  http://www.bartleby.com/268/7/44.html
Otto von Bismarck:
http://www.emersonkent.com/speeches/blood_and_
  iron.htm
Abraham Lincoln:
  http://www.bartleby.com/124/pres32.html
Patrick Pearse:
  http://www.emersonkent.com/speeches/ireland_
  unfree_shall_never_be_at_peace.htm
Dragutin Gavrilović:
  http://www.cacakmuzej.org.rs/wpcontent/uploads/
  2012/06/Wars-1804-19411.pdf
Robert Laird Borden:
http://www.collectionscanada.gc.ca/primeministers/
  h4-4069-e.html
David Lloyd George: Inglis, James *The War of Words*
  (Pier 9, 2010)
Vladimir Lenin:
http://www.marxists.org/archive/lenin/works/1919/
  mar/x06.htm
Woodrow Wilson:
  http://wwi.lib.byu.edu/index.php/Wilson's_War_
  Message_to_Congress
Emperor Haile Selassie I:
https://www.mtholyoke.edu/acad/intrel/selassie.htm

Dolores Ibárruri:
http://www.english.illinois.edu/maps/scw/farewell.htm
Adolf Hitler:
  http://fcit.usf.edu/holocaust/resource/document/
  HITLER1.htm
Winston Churchill:
  http://www.winstonchurchill.org/learn/speeches/
  speeches-of-winston-churchill/1940-finest-
  hour/128-we-shall-fight-on-the-beaches
Charles de Gaulle:
http://www.guardian.co.uk/theguardian/2007/apr/2
  9/greatspeeches1
Franklin D. Roosevelt:
  http://millercenter.org/scripps/archive/speeches/
  detail/3324
Joseph Stalin:
http://www.ibiblio.org/pha/timeline/411107awp.html
Joseph Goebbels:
http://www.calvin.edu/academic/cas/gpa/goeb36.htm
Mao Zedong:
  http://www.marxists.org/reference/archive/mao/
  selected-works/volume-3/mswv3_19.htm
Ho Chi Minh:
https://facultystaff.richmond.edu/~ebolt/history398/
  DeclarationOfIndependence-DRV.html
Golda Meir: Whiticker, Alan J. *Speeches that Reshaped
  the World* (New Holland, 2009)
Syngman Rhee: State security and regime security by

SOURCES

Yong-Pyo Hong (Palgrave) and
  http://trove.nla.gov.au/ndp/del/article/18431808
Sheikh Mujibur Rahman: The World's Greatest
  Speeches by Vijaya Kumar (Sterling)
Salvador Allende: Whiticker, Alan J. *Speeches that
  Reshaped the World* (New Holland, 2009)
Ronald Reagan: Reagan, Ronald *The Greatest
  Speeches of Ronald Reagan* (NewsMax Media, 2003)

ACKNOWLEDGEMENTS

Winston Churchill: Reproduced with permission of
Curtis Brown, London on behalf of the Estate of Sir
Winston Churchill: Copyright © Winston S. Churchill

Joseph Goebbels: © C. Schacht, Germany; translation
reproduced with kind permission of Randall Bytwerk

The author and publishers would like to thank
Chatham House for permission to reproduce Adolf
Hitler: Extracts from Baynes, N. (1942) *The Speeches of
Adolf Hitler* (Reichstag speech)

With thanks also to The Reagan Foundation and the
Franklin D. Roosevelt Presidential Library